FROM WORRY TO
Worship

A 30-Day
Devotional Guide

JULIE MORRIS

New Hope Publishers
Birmingham, Alabama

New Hope® Publishers
P. O. Box 12065
Birmingham, AL 35202-2065
www.newhopepubl.com

Library of Congress Cataloging-in-Publication Data
Morris, Julie.
From worry to worship : a 30-day devotional guide / by Julie Morris.
p. cm.— (God help me series ; 1)
Includes bibliographical references.
ISBN 1-56309-754-0 (pbk.)
1. Worry-Religious aspects-Christianity. 2. Devotional calendars.
I. Title. II. Series.
BV4908.5.M677 2003
242—dc21
2003000088

Cover design by Righteous Planet Design, Inc.
Franklin, Tennessee

ISBN: 1-56309-754-0

N034113 • 0403 • 5M1

Acknowledgments

I would like to thank Ricci Waters,
my life-long friend, and Sarah Morris,
my precious daughter, for the help and
encouragement they gave me while I wrote
From Worry to Worship.

Table of Contents

Introduction

These are scary times we are living in. There are so many things to worry about. If you are like I was, worries swirl around in your head, taking turns tormenting you. Struggling against them is exhausting.

Maybe you feel, as I did, that you can't quit worrying. Even though I had been a Bible teacher for years, I still couldn't control my anxious thoughts. I worried because I couldn't stop worrying. I hated it when people told me to trust God because I didn't know *how* to trust Him. Where was the trust button I could push? I felt like a terrible Christian because I couldn't trust Him like "everyone else." I didn't realize that many people were secretly worrying behind their contented-Christian masks. I didn't realize there was an antidote to the worry that poisoned my thoughts.

The Antidote to Worry

I prayed earnestly for the Lord to help me stop worrying. Soon He gave me something huge to "practice not worrying" about. This was the biggest worry I had ever faced: My doctor saw something suspicious on my mammogram, and he wanted me to go to a surgeon right away.

The night before I went to the surgeon, I was so anxious I couldn't sleep. I turned on the TV to a religious channel. A choir was singing a soft melody, "We exalt Thee. We exalt Thee, O Lord." Over and over they sang those words. My mind joined in their song, and soon I found that my panic subsided. A blanket of peace covered me and I fell asleep.

Later, I woke up and fear gripped me again. I repeated the words that helped me before: "We exalt Thee. We exalt Thee . . . I exalt You . . . I exalt You, O Lord." And after a while I fell asleep again. I repeated this process several times during the night.

The next day, I was relieved to hear the surgeon say that I

didn't have cancer, but I never forgot the valuable lesson I learned that night: It is impossible to worry and worship at the same time. Praise is the antidote to panic!

15 Minutes a Day

This book will help you progress from worry to worship in one month by spending just 15 minutes a day. Each devotion will help you to apply God's Word to your specific worries.

This book will never shame you because you worry. Instead, it will give you practical tips that will help you to turn your worries to worship. These practical tips are sprinkled generously throughout the book. Don't feel you have to do all of the practical tips! Just choose a few to start doing to begin your journey.

I based the six chapters of this book on six of God's qualities found in Isaiah 40. Isaiah 40 paints beautiful word pictures of God that help us to praise Him. Here are the six chapters.

1. We praise God for His **presence**:
He is over us, next to us, and inside of us.

2. We praise God for His **power**:
Everything that happens to us passes through His fingers first.

3. We praise God for His **plan**:
God knows what He is doing.

4. We praise God for His **purpose**:
No pain is wasted in God's economy.

5. We praise God for His **prize**:
God will reward us.

6. We praise God for His **promises**:
His Word gives us something tangible to hold on to as we step out in faith.

Daily Sections

Each daily section includes the following parts that you can easily complete in 15 minutes:

- **Read About It**—a meditation on the verse in Isaiah 40 or parallel verse that explores the quality of God identified in that chapter.
- **Think About It**—practical information that will encourage you to apply that day's Bible verse to your worries.
- **Write About It**—a questionnaire that will help you recognize the source of your worries.
- **Pray About It**—a place for you to write a prayer. This section also includes my prayer of praise.
- **Do It**—a helpful tip that will encourage you to put the principles into action.

Group Study Guide

A brief Leader's Guide is included at the end of the book so you may use *From Worry to Worship* in a group setting—in Bible studies, support groups, Sunday school classes, in your neighborhood or with another friend or two. The Leader's Guide offers questions that focus on one chapter a week, for a total of six weeks. They will encourage you to grow spiritually, share honestly, and find support with other Christians.

Julie Morris would love to hear from you! Her address is
2663 Valleydale Road PMB 266
Birmingham, AL35244
or julie@worrytoworship.com

For additional resources and information about Julie's Worry to Worship seminars and retreats, check out the Website at

www.worrytoworship.com.

Chapter 1

God's Presence

Day 1

God the Father is over us.

Today's Verse

Isaiah 40:22 *"He sits enthroned above the circle of the earth, and its people are like grasshoppers."*

Read About It

Many of us have a "Grasshopper Theology." We think of God sitting so far above the earth that we look like grasshoppers to Him. We wouldn't admit we think that way. When we read the Bible we find wonderful passages about how God is with us and will help us. But deep down, a part of us doesn't really believe that, especially when troubles rise up like tidal waves before us. Our problems seem enormous, and God seems small and so far away.

In verse 22, as well as several others in Isaiah 40, God draws word pictures for us so we will be able to visualize His greatness. He is not telling us that He is far away; instead, He is describing His enormity and urging us to have a heavenly perspective—to rise with Him above our problems and recognize how great He is and how small our problems are.

As you read these word pictures in Isaiah 40, see if you can visualize just how great God is:

Isaiah 40:22
He sits enthroned above the circle of the earth,
  and its people are like grasshoppers.
He stretches out the heavens like a canopy,
  and spreads them out like a tent to live in.

Isaiah 40:12
Who has measured the waters
  in the hollow of his hand,
or with the breadth of his hand
  marked off the heavens?
Who has held the dust of the earth in a basket,
  or weighed the mountains on the scales
  and the hills in a balance?

Isaiah 40:15
Surely the nations are like a drop in a bucket;
  they are regarded as dust on the scales;
he weighs the islands as though they were fine dust.

Other people in Scripture had a Grasshopper Theology. For example, in Numbers 13, Moses and his people were ready to enter the land God had promised to them. Moses sent twelve men to spy on the land. Ten of the spies came back saying that the land was full of giants, and the people seemed like grasshoppers in comparison. The other two, Joshua and Caleb, looked at it from a heavenly perspective: they knew God is big enough to defeat any giants in the land. But those with the Grasshopper Theology wouldn't be convinced. Joshua and Caleb entered the Promised Land, but the others missed out.

I used to have a Grasshopper Theology. I let my worries get me down, but I am learning to have a heavenly perspective. When I praise my God for His greatness and remember that He is with me, my problems become like grasshoppers!

Meditation on a Heavenly Perspective

I remember that day so clearly. As I'm writing this I'm nine again and my ears are still ringing from the worst news in the world: My friends Barbara and Nancy told Peggy that they did not like me anymore. Of course, Peggy couldn't wait to share every detail of their gossip with me.

My dad planned to take the family to Grandma's house in his sleek blue Navion that afternoon. Although I loved to fly, I entered the airplane so loaded down with hurts that I was not looking forward to the trip. Nancy and Barbara's fiery words echoed in the roar of the engine. After we took off, I glanced out the window and noticed, as if for the first time, that everything on the ground was miniature. Like Monopoly houses placed carefully on the board, the lovely homes near the airport suddenly dwindled in stature and significance. As usual, Dad flew over our neighborhood; though a half-hour away by car, this detour took only a few minutes. Looking out the window, I strained to see if Barbara and Nancy were outside playing, but I was too far away.

When I looked at the vast horizon before me, it didn't seem to matter anymore. I had broader perspective—a heavenly one. It was like I could see the whole picture now—where I had been and where I was going—and I was no longer stuck in tiny details like the cutting words of two unfaithful friends. As we soared effortlessly to Grandma's house, I looked forward in happy anticipation to the hugs that awaited me and I was relieved to leave Barbara and Nancy behind.

Think About It

Do you have a Grasshopper Theology?

Yes___ No___ 1. Do you often find yourself overwhelmed by worries?

Yes___ No___ 2. Do you often feel defeated and say things to yourself such as, "I'll never be able to do that!"?

Yes___ No___   3. When you are worried about something, do you find it impossible to turn off your anxious thoughts?

Yes___ No___   4. Does God often seem distant to you?

If you answered *yes* to any of those questions, you might have a Grasshopper Theology. Continue reading and you will find out what to do about it.

Write About It

What are you worried about today? Put one check next to the things that worry you, two checks next to things that worry you a lot, and three checks next to the things that you worry about most.

_____ Terrorism, war   _____ Surrounded by ungodliness
_____ Money   _____ Other people's problems
_____ Old age, death   _____ Unknown future
_____ Health, appearance   _____ Mistakes in the past, guilt
_____ Getting along with others   _____ Can't stop bad habit
_____ Loved ones' poor choices   _____ What people think about me
_____ Not enough time   _____ Possessions—in disrepair
_____ Inadequacy   _____ Possessions—wanting more

Pray About It

Reflect on your problems in light of today's verse, and journey from worry to worship by having a heavenly perspective—praising God that He is with you and that He is bigger than any of your problems. Isaiah 40:22 *"He sits enthroned above the circle of the earth, and its people are like grasshoppers"*

Lord, I've been worrying about . . .

_____

_____

_____

Help me rise above these worries and praise You because. . .

_____

_____

_____

_____

God, I praise You for Your greatness. When I allow my thoughts to rise up with You, I am awestruck by Your majesty. I see my problems from Your eyes and I put things in their proper perspective. You are the creator and sustainer of the universe, yet You love me and are concerned about anything that concerns me. You don't want me to pretend that my problems don't exist. Instead, You want me to face them, praising You that You are far bigger than any of my problems and that You are with me, helping me deal with them one by one.

Do It

Next time a worry hits you, ask yourself, "Am I acting like I have a Grasshopper Theology?"

Day 2
God the Son is next to us.

Today's Verse

Isaiah 40:11 *"He tends his flock like a shepherd: He gathers the lambs in his arms and carries them close to his heart."*

Read About It

Have you ever held a squirming toddler? I took care of a friend's child last week so I can answer that question with a resounding YES! And it's frustrating. I wanted to take care of him, but he would have none of the help I tried to give. All he could think about was getting out of my arms so he could do his own thing. That is how many of us respond to our Shepherd as He tries to gather us in His arms.

Yesterday we looked at God the Father who is over us. Today we are going to focus on God the Son who is next to us. Isaiah describes Him as our Shepherd who gathers us into His arms and carries us close to His heart.

In John 10 Jesus describes Himself using the same metaphor.

Let's examine several verses in this chapter to see what Jesus says about being our Shepherd.

• *John 10:11* *"I am the good shepherd. The good
  shepherd lays down his life for the sheep."*

Stop to think for a minute about how blessed you are to have such a loving Shepherd who died to set you free—free from guilt, death, hopelessness, and fear of the things to come. When you think about what Jesus did for you on the cross, do your worries turn to worship?

• *John 10:3* *"He calls his own sheep by name and
  leads them out."*

Jesus has chosen you for His very own. He called you out from the others to have a personal relationship with you. He doesn't just tell you to go on ahead; He leads you out of your old way of living into the exciting new life He has for you. Are you letting Him lead you out . . . or are you wandering away?

• *John 10:27* *"My sheep listen to my voice; I know
  them, and they follow me."*

When Jesus talks to me, His voice isn't audible, but I sense it with spiritual ears. You might know what I'm talking about, but in case you don't, I'll explain how I know when the Lord is speaking to me.

Ways I know the Lord is speaking to me:

1. A thought comes into my mind that brings peace and certainty.
2. The significance of a verse in the Bible "leaps off the page" at me.
3. Words I read or hear stand out in significance. (Often my preacher's sermon or a book I "happen" to pick up will offer just the direction I had been seeking.)
4. Several people happen to mention the same thing to me and I feel God nudging me in that direction.

If any of these things don't agree with the Bible, I know right away they are not from God.

Do you recognize the Lord's voice? Do you follow His instructions? Jesus reassures us in John 10 that His sheep know His voice. We just have to practice listening—expecting to hear from Him and being willing to follow.

Think About It

Today we talked about eight qualities of our Shepherd and four qualities of His sheep. Each of these qualities will help us to go from worry to worship.

Our Shepherd
He lays down his life for us.
He tends to us.
He gathers us in his arms.
He carries us close to his heart.
He calls us by name.
He leads us out.
He knows us.
He gives us eternal life.

His Sheep
We are able to hear Him.
We follow Him.
We shall never perish.
No one can snatch us out of His hand.

Write About It ✏

Answer this questionnaire and see how you're doing in following your Shepherd.

Yes___ No___   1. Do you have doubts that you are a Christian and that Jesus died to save you?

Yes___ No___   2. Are you too focused on taking care of your own needs to let Jesus tend to you?

Yes___ No___   3. When Jesus tries to gather you in His arms to have a daily quiet time, do you try to squirm out because you are too busy?

Yes___ No___   4. When you are worried, do you focus on your problems instead of your Shepherd who wants to carry you though them?

Yes___ No___   5. Do you believe that Jesus is too busy with others to call you personally?

Yes___ No___   6. Are you stuck in the same place you were last year, unable or unwilling to let Jesus lead you out?

Yes___ No___   7. When you know that God is leading you to do something, do you often refuse to follow Him?

Yes___ No___   8. Do you try to win God's favor and earn your way into heaven?

If you had any *yes* answers, your Shepherd wants to teach you how to follow Him better. Don't worry about how much you have to learn. Jesus promises to lead you. He will even give you the willingness to follow if you ask Him. The most important thing is that you start learning and start following Him more closely. In order to do that, it will be very helpful for you to talk your *yes* answers over with your pastor, Sunday school teacher, or respected Christian friend. Why don't you do it this week?

Pray About It 🙏

Thank God for being your Shepherd. As you look at your answers to the questionnaire, write your prayer below, asking Him to help you to be a better lamb.

_____

_____

_____

_____

_____

_____

_____

Reflect on today's verse as you journey from worry to worship. Isaiah 40:11 *"He tends his flock like a shepherd: he gathers the lambs in his arms and carries them close to his heart."*

Lord, I praise You because You are my Shepherd. You love me just as I am. You laid down Your life for me. You want to spend time just being close to me. You want to lead me out of my old ways, and when things are too hard for me, You even offer to carry me. You speak to me in words that I can understand and promise that I will know Your voice . . . if I will listen. I come to You now with a new hope because my hope is in You, not myself. You are my Shepherd. You are with me and You will help me to follow You today and every day.

Do It 👣

Next time you are worried, don't be like a squirming lamb trying to get out of your Shepherd's arms. Hold Him tight and let Him carry you.

Day 3
God the Holy Spirit is inside us.

Today's Verse

Isaiah 40:29 *"He gives strength to the weary."*

Read About It

"Why do I continue to overeat when I want to lose weight more than anything in my life?" This question baffled me but didn't slow down my journey to the refrigerator. Something compelled me to do what I had just determined not to. It did not make sense. In almost everything else I was in control—I knew what I wanted to do and did it—but with food it was different.

Here I was, RN supervisor of a large medical-surgical floor telling people what to do to get healthy, and I couldn't lose the weight that made my blood pressure soar. Just that after-noon my doctor warned me to lose weight or I could have a stroke even though I was only in my 30s. I determined on the way home from the doctor's office that I would go back on my diet immediately. Well, tomorrow for sure. But now I needed a little something to calm my nerves . . .

I was tired of dealing with this problem. Fed up. Weary of the whole thing. How could I ever make the healthy lifestyle changes my doctor was insisting on?

I asked myself that question for the last time 20 years ago. God began to show me how to rely on His Holy Spirit one day at a time to lose my unhealthy extra pounds and keep them off. God has blessed me in unimaginable ways because of my weakness with food, not in spite of it. He turned the misery of all those years of failed diets and gained pounds into an exciting ministry when I became willing to step out in faith and follow His Spirit's leading. (I wrote the Step Forward series for people who want to lose weight by relying on the Lord. Step Forward's website is www.stepforwarddiet.com.)

The Holy Spirit is the third person of the Trinity. Some people don't understand how God can be Father, Son, and Holy Spirit—three, yet one. The Trinity is much easier to understand when you think of water. It is also three, yet one. It has the same components (H_2O), but is found in three different forms: water, ice, and steam.

The Greek word for helper is *parakletos*, which means "intercessor, consoler, advocate, comforter." Just think about it. The Holy Spirit lives inside of us to help us with everything! When we are weary, He gives us strength. When we are worried, He gives us peace . . . if we let Him. Keep studying *From Worry to Worship* to learn more about how to rely on the Holy Spirit.

Think About It

The Holy Spirit helps us with everything we do . . . if we rely on Him.	Yes___ No___ Do you pray for help before doing something challenging and also while doing it?
The Holy Spirit gives us guidance . . . if we listen.	Yes___ No___ Do you pray for guidance with each important decision you have to make?
The Holy Spirit helps us to share our faith with others . . . if we will do it.	Yes___ No___ Do you share your faith with others, confident that the Holy Spirit will help you to do it?
The Holy Spirit teaches us and counsels us . . . if we listen to Him.	Yes___ No___ Do you listen to what you know God is telling you to do?

The Holy Spirit gives us exciting gifts—talents and abilities that glorify God . . . if we will use them.	Yes___ No___ Do you know what special ability the Holy Spirit has given you? (If not, ask your pastor for a Spiritual Gift Inventory.)
The Holy Spirit gives us wonderful qualities . . . if we stay close to Him.	Yes___ No___ Are you experiencing the fruit of the Spirit today: Love, joy, peace, patience, kindness, goodness, faithfulness, gentleness and self-control?

Write About It

Which *no* answer is God leading you to deal with today? What can you do to turn your *no* to a *yes*? (If you don't know, pray about it and ask your pastor, Sunday school teacher, or respected Christian friend.)

_____

_____

_____

_____

Pray About It

Today's Verse: Isaiah 40:29 *"He gives strength to the weary."*
Tell God about things that are making you weary today. Journey from worry to worship by praising God for the Holy Spirit, which is inside of you to help you in these areas.

_____

_____

_____

_____

Lord, thank You for putting Your Holy Spirit inside of me the minute I accepted Jesus as my Savior. Thank You, too, that because of what Jesus did on the cross, You promise never to take the Holy Spirit away from me. And thank You that, through the power of the Holy Spirit, I can overcome any problem I have without becoming weary. Help me to rely on Him more.

Do It

Next time you are weary, praise God that His Holy Spirit is inside of you to help you at that very moment.

Day 4

God is with us.

Today's Verse

Deuteronomy 33:12 *"Let the beloved of the Lord rest secure in him, for he shields him all day long, and the one the Lord loves rests between his shoulders."*

Read About It

I received a phone call telling me about the destruction of the World Trade Center while I was writing a meditation on this Scripture one quiet Tuesday morning. It amazed me how the word picture in this passage came alive after I hung up the phone. During the terrifying days that followed, I clung to this verse and was able to rest secure in the Lord. Years ago I would not have been able to do that because I was convinced that I shouldn't be called God's beloved.

When you read, "Let the beloved of the Lord . . . " did you exclude yourself from the wonderful promises of rest and protection that follow because you don't feel that you are God's beloved? Think about your answer before going on. (If you feel sure that you are God's beloved, you may skip to the next section.)

If you don't really believe that you are God's beloved, you have a huge roadblock in the way of your relationship, but it is not too big for God's Word to overcome. Let's get to work and knock this roadblock down! Use these three passages to overcome the lie that you are not God's beloved.

1. John 1:12 *"Yet to all who received him, to those who believed in his name, he gave the right to become children of God."*
Have you received Christ as your Savior? Do you believe in His name? Jesus means the Lord saves. Do you believe that Jesus came to save you from your sins? If so, He has given you the right to become God's beloved child.

2. 1 John 1:9 *"If we confess our sins, he is faithful and just and will forgive us our sins and purify us from all unrighteousness."*
Jesus died to save you from your sins. And when you confess your sins, God forgives you completely and makes you pure and holy.

3. Colossians 1:21-22 *"Once you were alienated from God and were enemies in your minds because of your evil behavior. But now he has reconciled you by Christ's physical body through death to present you holy in his sight, without blemish and free from accusation."*
Because Jesus is your Savior, you are reconciled to God. Your disobedience builds walls that try to separate you, but when you come to God with genuine repentance, He forgives you every time. He does not keep score or kick you out of the family because you have sinned one too many times.

Think About It

Are you being disobedient to the Lord in some area? Stop for a minute and ask Him to show you any sin you have been committing. Don't strain trying to remember every sin you have ever committed. Just confess the things the Lord brings to mind right now.

Write About It

List the sins that the Lord brings to your mind and ask God to forgive you for them.

_____

_____

_____

_____

Pray About It

Write a prayer thanking Jesus for tearing down the walls that your sins built up between you. Thank Him that there is nothing standing between you and God. You are His beloved child. Now you can experience His love fully.

_____

_____

_____

_____

_____

Reflect on today's verse as you journey from worry to worship. Deuteronomy 33:12 *"Let the beloved of the Lord rest secure in him for he shields him all day long, and the one the Lord loves rests between his shoulders."*

Lord, I praise You that because of what Jesus did for me on the cross, I know that I am Your beloved child and I can rest secure in You. Help me each day to walk in Your ways so that I will experience Your promises of rest and protection. Thank You that when I remember that I am Your beloved child and that You are with me all day (and night!) long, I am able to go from worry to worship.

Do It

Next time you are worried, don't be like a squirming lamb trying to get out of your Shepherd's arms. Hold Him tight and let Him carry you.

Day 5
God is with us.

Today's Verse

Zephaniah 3:17 *"The Lord your God is with you, he is mighty to save. He will take great delight in you, he will quiet you with his love, he will rejoice over you with singing."*

Read About It

When I read this verse I think of my grandmother. She was 40 when my mom was born, so to me, my precious Grandma was always old.

I loved to spend the night at Grandma's house where I felt so loved and secure. Many fond memories of her still make me smile 50 years later, but my favorite is sleeping in her big, creaky antique bed. Since she didn't have a guestroom in her tiny house, she and I had to share the bed, and before going to sleep we always held hands and talked. Her hand was a lot like mine is now, skinny, with long fingers and veins clearly visible, weaving together under paper-like skin.

The lonely sound of a train whistle often serenaded us as Grandma talked about what her life was like when she was a little girl. She would sing songs to me that her grandmother sang to her when she was my age, like "Go Tell Aunt Rhody The Old Gray Goose Is Dead." For some reason, that song made me feel good. I guess it was because Grandma was singing it to me.

My Grandma loved me, and I felt safe with her in that old bed. Her love quieted all my fears of my abusive father and feelings of inferiority that surrounded me at home. I knew that, no matter what anyone else thought about me, she took delight in me. And she rejoiced over me with singing.

Grandma's love gave me a little taste of what God's love for me is like. The Lord is with me, and when I remember that, I feel safe. When I let Him, He quiets me with His love and rejoices over me with singing.

Lord, help me to remember that today and always!

Think About It

In this chapter we have talked about God's reassuring presence: God the Father is over us, the Son is next to us, the Holy Spirit is inside us. Yesterday we discussed what keeps us from rejoicing in God's presence: our disobedience. Today we will look at something else that keeps us from rejoicing in God's presence: the "Yes buts."

Has anyone ever said to you, "Yes. I know you're right, but . . ."? Sometimes that comment is followed by a legitimate question or concern, but often it is followed by an excuse. Let me demonstrate:

- When I encouraged Mary to spend a few minutes having a quiet time every morning, her answer to me was, "Yes, but I don't have time."
- When Sue told her husband that the grass needed mowing, his answer to her was, "Yes, but I don't feel like mowing the grass."

Often when we read the Bible, we say "Yes, but . . ." to God. When we do that, we are rejecting His truth and giving ourselves permission to believe a lie.

Let's look again at today's verse along with some Yes, but's that refute each of the promises found there. After each Yes, there is a parallel passage that reinforces today's verse. Put a check next to any *Yes, but* that you might say.

	The Promises in Zephaniah 3:17	The Yes, but . . .	A Parallel Passage
	The Lord is with you.	Yes, but . . . I feel far away from Him.	**Psalm 118:6** "The Lord is with me; I will not be afraid. What can man do to me?"
	He is mighty to save.	Yes, but . . . I'm sure He is too busy to bother with my small problems.	**Isaiah 41:13** "For I am the Lord, your God, who takes hold of your right hand and says to you, Do not fear; I will help you."
	He will quiet you with his love.	Yes, but . . . the only time I'm not worried is when I'm too busy to think.	**Matthew 11:28** [Jesus said] "Come to me all you who are weary and burdened, and I will give you rest."
	He will rejoice over you with singing.	Yes, but . . . He can't rejoice over me because I'm not good enough.	**Isaiah 49:15-16** "Can a mother forget the baby at her breast and have no compassion on the child she has borne? Though she may forget, I will not forget you! See, I have engraved you on the palms of my hands."

Write About It

What *Yes, but* have you told God? Write the promise here that you questioned. Ask God to help you to believe His Word completely.

_____

_____

_____

_____

_____

_____

Pray About It

Reflect on today's verse as you journey from worry to worship. Zephaniah 3:17 *"The Lord your God is with you, he is mighty to save. He will take great delight in you, he will quiet you with his love, he will rejoice over you with singing."*

Lord, I praise You for Your presence. You are with me every minute of every day and all through the night as well. Even though I don't deserve Your love, You give it to me freely. I praise You for loving me just as I am. When I think of Zephaniah 3:17, the hardness in my heart melts and I rejoice over You because You are rejoicing over me. I will not say, "Yes, but . . ." to You. Instead, I will praise You that You care enough about me to stay by my side, to save me, to quiet me with Your love and to rejoice over me with singing. You are such a precious God . . . and I praise You!

Do It

Don't tell God, "Yes, but . . ."!

Chapter 2

God's Power

Day 6

Everything that happens to us passes through God's fingers first.

Today's Verse

Isaiah 40:10 *"See, the Sovereign Lord comes with power, and his arm rules for him."*

Read About It

Have you ever had tea with royalty? Have you gone to lunch with the president or sat down to chat with a foreign head of state? I haven't. But I am sure that if I did, I would be very careful to show these world rulers the respect that they deserve.

Yet there are times when I have stood up the King of kings. I have ignored His presence and tossed aside the letters He wrote to me over thousands of years. I have known what He wanted me to do, but insisted on doing my own thing anyway. I have taken His love for granted, doubted His Word, complained about His gifts, and demanded more and more of His blessings. I have forgotten who He is—the sovereign

Lord—creator and ruler of the entire universe.

Even kings have no power except for that which God gives them. Isaiah 40:23–24 explains this:

He brings princes to naught
and reduces the rulers of this world to nothing.
No sooner are they planted,
no sooner are they sown,
no sooner do they take root in the ground,
than he blows on them and they wither,
and a whirlwind sweeps them away like chaff.
Isaiah 40:23–24

God is not only sovereign over kings and nations; He is sovereign over individuals. Everything that happens to us passes through God's fingers first. There is no such thing as "luck." God is in control.

Think About It

Think about this: Why does focusing on God's sovereignty help you not to worry?

_____

_____

_____

_____

Habakkuk helps us to find the answer. He lived in uncertain times, even worse than we are living in now. His country was being threatened by Babylon, and he realized that if Judah were captured, many would be killed and there would be famine in the land. But Habakkuk went from worry to worship. Let's find out how he did it by looking at the following passage:

Habakkuk 3:17–18 *"Though the fig tree does not bud and there are no grapes on the vines, though the olive crop fails and the fields produce no food, though there are no sheep in the pen and no cattle in the stalls, yet I will rejoice in the Lord, I will be joyful in God my Savior."*

Habakkuk lists all of his concerns and commits to praise the Lord anyway. It really helps to put our worries on paper. Review your list of worries from Day One. In the space below, rephrase Habakkuk's list of worries, found in Habakkuk 3:17–18, putting your biggest worries in place of his. (For instance, "Though I may lose my job and we might not have enough money to pay the bills. . . .") Make a commitment to rejoice in the Lord, no matter what happens—to praise Him for His presence and His power.

Lord,
When worries attack me, I commit to rejoice in You—to praise You for Your presence and Your power instead of focusing on my worries. Even if the following worries happen:

_____
_____
_____

I commit to rejoice in You—because You are my Savior.

Signed _____ *Date* _____

Habakkuk turns his worries to worship by reminding himself of God's sovereignty and sufficiency: ***Habakkuk 3:19*** *"The Sovereign Lord is my strength; he makes my feet like the feet of a deer, He enables me to go on the heights."*

Because God is sovereign and has all power, Habakkuk can rest, strengthened by this life-changing thought: **Though he doesn't know what his future holds, he knows Who holds his future!** He knows that God will transform him so that he can stand up in difficult, frightening places, and he is confident that God will empower him to do anything that he needs to do.

David had that same confidence. He tells us about it in Psalm 18. Notice that David also speaks of deer feet. I didn't fully understand until I saw deer, in a documentary about the Holy Lands, standing precariously on craggy mountain ledges. One false step and they would plunge to their deaths.

Psalm 18:32–36 *"It is God who arms me with strength and makes my way perfect. He makes my feet like the feet of a deer; he enables me to stand on the heights. He trains my hands for battle; my arms can bend a bow of bronze. You give me your shield of victory, and your right hand sustains me; you stoop down to make me great. You broaden the path beneath me, so that my ankles do not turn."*

Write About It

Yes___ No___   1. Are you confident, like Habakkuk and David, that God controls your future?

Yes___ No___   2. Do you try to distract yourself from your worry by becoming too busy to think about them?

Yes___ No___   3. Do you often pretend that you don't have worries because you want others to think you have it all together?

Yes___ No___   4. Do you numb your worry with behaviors like overeating, watching TV, shopping, surfing the Internet?

Yes___ No___   5. Are you often so busy worrying about yesterday and tomorrow that you don't enjoy today?

Yes___ No___ 6. Do you often take God for granted and forget that He is the King of kings?

Yes___ No___ 7. While you are in the midst of trials, do you often forget that God can save you?

Yes___ No___ 8. Have you been able to do things or endure things that you thought you never could?

Yes___ No___ 9. Do you give God the credit for this?

Yes___ No___ 10. When you look back at how God has changed you, do you to go from worry to worship?

Write about a time when you were able to do things or endure things that you never thought you could.

_____

_____

_____

_____

Pray About It 🙏

As you look at your questionnaire, write a prayer asking God to help you in the needed areas. If you are pleased with your answers, praise God for His help.

_____

_____

_____

_____

Reflect on today's verse as you journey from worry to worship. Isaiah 40:10 *"See, the Sovereign Lord comes with power, and his arm rules for him."*

Lord, thank You for being my Sovereign Lord. Help me to remember that You are in control. Even if I can't see Your hand at work or understand what You are doing, help me to praise You for Your power and Your presence. When worries come, help me to remember that I have a choice: I don't have to worry myself sick. Instead, I can praise You for Your power at work in the world and Your power at work in me. When I praise You, I will journey from worry to worship.

Do It

Next time worries attack you, praise God for His sovereignty and say, "I don't know what my future holds, but I know Who holds my future."

Day 7

Everything that happens to us passes through God's fingers first.

Today's Verse

Philippians 4:6–7 *"Do not be anxious about anything, but in everything, by prayer and petition, with thanksgiving, present your requests to God. And the peace of God, which transcends all understanding, will guard your hearts and your minds in Christ Jesus."*

Read About It 📖

I loved my mother very much. From the time I was a little girl, I can remember thinking that I would never be able to bear it if she died. During my childhood I often got up in the middle of the night to tiptoe into her room and make sure she was breathing.

Years later, after I had moved to Florida, it happened. I got the call I had been dreading for a lifetime. My mother had suffered a severe stroke and was in a hospital far away in Virginia. According to the doctor, this vibrant woman, who had always been there to help me with every problem I faced and cheer me on, would either die or be a total invalid.

I was devastated. I prayed and prayed, but I couldn't stop crying. I knew from Philippians 4:7 about the peace that God promised, so I kept silently screaming out to Him, "Where is the peace You promised?" But it didn't come.

That night after I arrived at the hospital, I lay near my mother on a lumpy hospital lounge chair begging God for two miracles: healing for my precious mother and peace for me. Both seemed impossible. My mother's stroke was too severe and my worries too overwhelming. Worries swarmed in my brain like bees on a hive that had just been shaken. How could I take care of my mother in Virginia and my family in Florida? How could I live without my mother? What would happen to my father? Around and around my worries flew—unceasingly . . . uncontrollably.

Sometime during that unending night I realized what might be blocking my peace: I had been focusing on the promise of peace in Philippians 4:7, but had forgotten the command that goes with that promise. In Philippians 4:6, God says to pray with thanksgiving! So I started giving thanks. Thanks for the caring nurses. Thanks that I could be there with my mother. Thanks that my boss had said that I could have as much time off as I needed. Soon my thanksgiving started changing its focus. I said, *Thank You, God, that Jeremiah 29:11 tells me that You have plans to profit my mother, not to harm her. Thank You that though I don't know what my future holds, I know You hold my future. Thank You that You promised not to give Mom, my family, and me more pain than we could bear. Thank You that You are close to the brokenhearted.* I was exhausted, but I continued to pray and give thanks.

Around 5:00, as that sleepless night drew to a close, one of the miracles began to happen. Peace started peeping through in my heart as the first light of dawn touched the morning sky. Mother was in a coma and would soon go to be with the Lord. The miracle of healing that I had prayed for would not happen. But the worries that had attacked me all night were gone. I felt confident that God would help me, one day at a time, to get through the grieving that waited for me. He would fill the emptiness that my mother's death would leave. He would be there to help me with my problems. And He would be my encourager and my comforter.

As if to confirm my newfound hope, I remembered the words on a wall hanging I had purchased impulsively while shopping the week before Mother's stroke. I realized that God had been preparing me for this tragedy.

The words said: "A head hung in despair cannot scan the horizon for God's provision." The message was that my peace would not come until I started looking up and praising the Lord. *And it was right.*

Think About It

Everyone tormented by worries wants peace. But as I learned, we will not have peace during troubled times unless we have a thankful heart. I recently discovered a passage that confirms this important concept. The command in 1 Thessalonians 5:18 is familiar, *"Give thanks in all circumstances, for this is God's will for you in Christ Jesus."* But the command in the next verse is often ignored: *"Do not put out the Spirit's fire."*

Have you thought about what that means? It means that if we don't give thanks in all things (even in tragic things), our lack of thanksgiving will be like a wet blanket on the Spirit inside of us, and our spiritual fruit will wither and become rotten. The third fruit of the Spirit, listed in Galatians 5:22, is peace. For those of us who struggle with worry, this is a life-changing message! God's power is in us to help us overcome destructive things like worry, but without thanksgiving (and its very close first cousin, praise) we will put out the Spirit's fire and His power at work in us will be quenched.

Write About It 🖋

Is your lack of thanksgiving putting out the Spirit's fire in you? Check your spiritual fruit. In the left column you will find the fruit of the Spirit listed in Galatians 5:22–23. In the other three columns, you will find rotten fruit. **Circle any rotten fruit that you see in your life.**

Fruit of the Spirit	Rotten Fruit		
Love	Hatred	Resentment	Bitterness
Joy	Sadness	Shame	Self-pity
Peace	Fear	Discontentment	Critical spirit
Patience	Rushing	Overbusyness	Irritability
Kindness	Rudeness	Selfishness	Self-centeredness
Goodness	Unrighteousness	Defiance	Rebellion
Faithfulness	Unreliability	Giving in	Giving up
Gentleness	Gruffness	Harshness	Raging
Self-Control	Impulsiveness	Compulsiveness	Overindulging

Do you have any rotten fruit? There are many reasons why you may not experience the fruit of the Spirit. Maybe you are not thankful in all circumstances, as 1 Thessalonians 5:18 commands. Change that by making a thanksgiving list.

Make a thanksgiving list simply by making a list of things you are thankful for. Every time you are upset, make one of these lists—the more worries you have, the longer your list should be. If it's a bad day, you may decide to write thirty things you are thankful for. It really helps. Try it! See how many thanksgivings you can list in five minutes.

Pray About It

Confess any rotten fruit you have discovered in your life and ask God to replace it with His fruit of the Spirit. Confess ways you have put a wet blanket on His Spirit's fire, such as by not praying or not giving thanks in all circumstances.

_____

_____

_____

_____

Reflect on today's verse as you journey from worry to worship. Philippians 4:6–7 *"Do not be anxious about anything, but in everything, by prayer and petition, with thanksgiving, present your requests to God. And the peace of God, which transcends all understanding, will guard your hearts and your minds in Christ Jesus."*

God, thank You for Your power at work in me through the Holy Spirit. Because of Your Spirit, I am not at the mercy of my fears. Through Your Spirit's power I can go from worry to worship and my panic will turn to peace. When I cooperate with You by praying and giving thanks, Your Spirit produces wonderful fruit in me, filling my heart and mind with peace, no matter how difficult my circumstances. Now that I know what to do when fear strikes, I no longer have to live being afraid of being afraid.

Do It

Next time you have a long list of worries, make a thanksgiving list that's even longer!

Day 8

*Everything that happens to us
passes through God's fingers first.*

Today's Verse

Matthew 6:31–33 *"So do not worry, saying, 'What shall we eat?' or 'What shall we drink?' or 'What shall we wear?' For the pagans run after all these things, and your heavenly Father knows that you need them. But seek first his kingdom and his righteousness, and all these things will be given to you as well."*

Read About It

We have been talking about God's power for the past two days. The first day we talked about our sovereign Lord who gives us power. The second day we talked about something that blocks His power: lack of thanksgiving. Today we will focus on something else that blocks God's power at work in our lives: focusing on our problems instead of God.

Think About It

In today's passage, Jesus talks gently and compassionately to those of us who tend to worry. He shares godly principles that will help us to turn our worries to worship. Look at His entire message by reading Matthew 6:25–34. Then let's look at five principles Jesus is teaching us through these verses.

1. Don't major on the minors. Matthew 6:25 *"Do not worry about your life . . . ."* A minister from Romania told my minister one day, "I am concerned about you Americans. You are so worried about all of your many possessions that you don't have time to think about the really important things." That's a good point. We have so much "stuff." Everything we own can own us if we are not careful.

2. Don't forget you are the King's kid! Matthew 6:26, 28–32 *" . . . your heavenly father knows you need them."* Jesus draws such beautiful word pictures for us about trusting God. Too often we forget that we are God's precious children. We scurry around trying to gather up things that will make us feel secure, but God's children don't need to do that. All of our things will not bring true security because they can vanish in a matter of seconds. The only true security comes when we trust our Heavenly Father.

3. Don't waste your days worrying. Matthew 6:27 *"Who of you by worring can add a single hour to his life?"* Because of worry, people not only waste hours, but entire lives. Most of us know that worry may lead to problems such as strokes, heart attacks, and ulcers. Worrying also encourages the secretion of stress hormones, such as cortisol, and these hormones diminish the effectiveness of the immune system so that worriers are more receptive to colds, flu, autoimmune diseases, and even cancer!

4. Put first things first. Matthew 6:33 *"But seek first his Kingdom and his righteousness . . . ."* Jesus tells us that there are two things we need to seek before everything else: God's kingdom and His righteousness. We seek God's kingdom by abiding with the Lord and focusing on Him instead of worldly things. We seek God's righteousness in two ways: by trusting Jesus' sacrifice on the cross to make us right with God, and by cooperating with the Holy Spirit as He enables us to obey God.

5. Live one day at a time. Matthew 6:34 *"Each day has enough trouble of it's own."* Tomorrow never really arrives. Yesterday is gone forever. We need to work on changing the things we can change today and leaving yesterday and tomorrow in God's hands. When we begin living one day at a time in this way, our lives are changed and we go from worry to worship.

The "Serenity Prayer" by Reinhold Niebuhr (adapted) describes this lifestyle so beautifully:

God,
grant me the serenity
to accept the things
I cannot change,
the courage to change
the things I can,
and the wisdom
to know the difference.

Write About It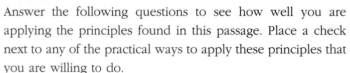

Answer the following questions to see how well you are applying the principles found in this passage. Place a check next to any of the practical ways to apply these principles that you are willing to do.

Principle Jesus Is Teaching Us	Am I Presently Applying That Principle?	Practical Way to Apply the Principle
Don't major on the minors.	1. Do you have a quiet time almost every day? Yes___ No___	Spend 15 minutes a day praying and studying God's Word.
Don't forget that you are the King's kid!	2. Do you believe the lie that you are insignificant to God, or that He is too busy with more important people? Yes___ No___	Write a Father's Day card to God thanking Him for being your *Abba*. (*Abba* means *"daddy."* See Mark 14:36.) Mention specific blessings He has given you.
Don't waste your days worrying.	3. Do you waste a lot of time worrying each day? Yes___ No___ 4. Do you have physical problems that could be attributed to worry? Yes___ No___	Write a reassuring Scripture on an index card. Every time you catch yourself worrying, say, **"Stop."** Then take your card out and focus on the Scripture.
Put first things first.	5. If during the last 24 hours someone had recorded your thoughts, what would that person say was most important to you? Yes___ No___	Buy tapes or CDs of someone reading the Bible. Keep them in your car so they turn on automatically every time you drive.
Live one day at a time.	6. Do you work at living one day at a time? Yes___ No___	Remember this saying: "When you try to carry yesterday's regrets and tomorrow's burdens, you will miss out on the joys of today."

Here is another important question: What have you worried about that never happened?

_____

_____

_____

Pray About It

Consider your answers to the questions above. Ask God to help you to do the things you checked so that you can go from worry to worship.

_____

_____

_____

_____

Reflect on today's verse as you journey from worry to worship. Matthew 6:31–33 *"So do not worry, saying, 'What shall we eat?' or 'What shall we drink?' or 'What shall we wear?' For the pagans run after all these things, and your heavenly Father knows that you need them. But seek first his kingdom and his righteousness, and all these things will be given to you as well."*

Lord, everything I need comes from You. I am open to receive it. I face this day and all of life knowing that You will provide for my needs. Please help me to make You Lord over everything in my life. Give me the desire and ability to do Your will, and the faith to believe that You are my Abba, and You love me. Help me each day to live in Your kingdom, basking in Your sufficiency.

Do It

Live one day at a time!

Day 9
*Everything that happens to us
passes through God's fingers first.*

Today's Verse

Matthew 11:28–29 *[Jesus said] "Come to me,
all you who are weary and burdened, and I
will give you rest. Take my yoke upon you and
learn from me, for I am gentle and humble in
heart, and you will find rest for your souls."*

Read About It

Are you weary and burdened by your problems? If you are,
you're worried! The Hebrew word for worry is *amal*, and the
Greek word is *ponos*. They mean "heavy labor, toil, anguish,
misery, distress, weariness."

Do those words describe you? If they do, you need to listen
to Jesus' words in today's verse. He invites you to yoke yourself to Him. You will miss out on His beautiful word picture
unless you understand what kind of yoke He is talking about.
A yoke is like a wooden collar that an animal wears when
plowing the fields. It looks like an upside down "u." Since
long before Jesus' time, people have been training young
oxen by yoking one of them together with an older, more
experienced ox. That double yoke looks like a lopsided "m,"
with one side larger than the other. It joins the two oxen
together. The young one walks alongside the older one, while
the older ox carries most of the load.

Jesus tells you if you're weary and burdened to come to Him and He will give you rest. If you take up His yoke and walk alongside Him, He will carry most of the load.

Think About It

Do you want to know how to yoke yourself to Jesus? Here are three ways, and the Scriptures that help us understand them.

1. Tell Jesus how much you need His help.

In John 15:5, Jesus says, "I am the vine; you are the branches. If a man remains in me and I in him, he will bear much fruit; *apart from me you can do nothing.*"

2. Ask Jesus to show you how you pull away from Him.

Lamentations 3:40 says, "Let us examine our ways and test them, and let us return to the Lord."

3. Surrender your will and your life to Jesus.

In Romans 12:1, Paul urges us to "offer your bodies as living sacrifices, holy and pleasing to God. This is your spiritual act of worship."

Write About It

Let's explore some practical things that we can do to be yoked to Jesus. To stay yoked to Jesus, we need to aim to do these things throughout each day. Be encouraged by Jesus' words in the verse that follows today's verse. He says, "My yoke is easy and my burden is light."

Once we learn how wonderful it is to be yoked to Jesus, it is easier to do things that will help us to stay that way. Here are some practical ways to yoke ourselves to Jesus. Write your own ideas in the spaces provided.

Tell Him how much you need His help.

1. Before you open your eyes each morning, tell Jesus you need His help that day.

2. Have a quiet time for a few minutes first thing in the morning. List challenges you face that day. Ask Jesus to help you.

3. Any time you face a challenge, whisper a little prayer asking Jesus for His help.

4. Memorize Philippians 4:13— "I can do all things through Christ who strengthens me" (NKJV). Say this verse several times a day, whenever you need it.

5. _____

6. _____

Ask Jesus to show you ways you pull away from Him.

Draw a check mark next to any of these statements that describe the ways that you pull away from Jesus:

_____ 1. Fretting instead of praying, focusing on problems instead of Him.

_____ 2. Being too busy to remember Jesus is there.

_____ 3. Disobeying what you know Jesus wants you to do.

_____ 4. Complaining and feeling sorry for yourself instead of giving thanks.

_____ 5. Blaming others and holding a grudge.

_____ 6. Ignoring the hand that Jesus holds out to you because you feel unworthy.

_____ 7. Other _____

Surrender your will and your life to Him.

Pray about it. Offer God your life and tell him that you want His will. Ask Him to help you to change any areas you checked above.

_____

_____

_____

_____

Pray About It

Reflect on today's verse as you journey from worry to worship. Matthew 11:28–29 *[Jesus said] "Come to me, all you who are weary and burdened, and I will give you rest. Take my yoke upon you and learn from me, for I am gentle and humble in heart, and you will find rest for your souls."*

Jesus, I want to be yoked to You. I want to experience Your rest in my life. I'm tired of being tired, Lord. I am so weary. I need Your help. Help me to take up Your yoke now. Help me not to pull away and run off on my own, trying to do things in my own power. Help me, Jesus, to surrender my will to You and experience Your freedom as I walk daily with You.

Do It

When you feel weary, it is probably because you got out of your yoke. Yoke yourself back to Jesus!

Day 10

Everything that happens to us passes through God's fingers first.

Today's Verse

2 Corinthians 12:9 *"My grace is sufficient for you, for my power is made perfect in weakness."*

Read About It

Do you want to know the things about me that God has used? My weaknesses! The reason I am able to write this book is because He is helping me to overcome my weakness with worry. I wrote the *Step Forward* series—Bible studies with an emphasis on losing weight—because of the things I learned in overcoming my weakness with food. I am able to counsel people who suffer from depression because a few years ago when my hormones went wacky, I went through a depression, and eventually came out of it victoriously.

With each of my weaknesses, I have learned how to rely on God's strength, so rather than being a detriment, the weakness has turned out to be a blessing. I know that now as I look back, but when I was in the midst of it, especially my 30-year struggle with compulsive eating, my weakness seemed something that I needed to be ashamed of, rather than something that would end up blessing me. That is because I didn't understand what God was saying in today's verse.

In 2 Corinthians 12:9, God is telling us that His grace is sufficient for us, but I didn't understand the full meaning of grace. I wonder if you do.

What do you think God's grace is?

_____

_____

_____

_____

Think About It

I learned in church that grace is God's unmerited favor of us. This means that there is nothing I can do to deserve God's favor. I can't do anything to make God love me, because He already does. And I can't work my way to heaven, but I know I am going there because of the grace God gives to all Christians.

Ephesians 2:8–9 tells us about this wonderful aspect of His grace: *"It is by grace you have been saved, through faith—and this not from yourselves, it is the gift of God—not by works, so that no one can boast."* When we stop to think about it, grace is a pretty amazing gift!

But that is only half of what grace is. Another verse gives us the other half of the definition of grace. It's 2 Corinthians 9:8: *"God is able to make all grace abound to you, so that in all things at all times, having all that you need, you will abound in every good work."*

Let's look more closely at this exciting, life-changing promise. It says that God will provide His power to us. Not just a little power—He will make it abundant in each of us—so that:
• In all things (even with things as hard as trusting God with every problem we face.)
• At all times (even when we are bombarded by problems and can't get our minds off of them.)
• Having all that we need (God promises to provide everything that we need.)
• We will abound in every good work. (There's that word *abound* again. That doesn't mean "just enough," but "more than we can even ask or imagine.")

Amazing Grace!
Let's look at the complete definition of grace in light of 2 Corinthians 9:8. *"God is able to make all grace abound to you, so that in all things at all times, having all that you need, you will abound in every good work."*

Grace is not just God's unmerited favor of me.
It is also His _____ _____ in me.
(Figure out what the two blanks are before going any further.)

> *Grace is God's unmerited favor of me and His unlimited power in me.*

Try to memorize that definition because it will help you every day of your life.

Now let's look at today's verse again. 2 Corinthians 12:9 *"My grace is sufficient for you, for my power is made perfect in weakness."* Do you understand why our weaknesses are blessings? Because they help us lean on God more. When we look to God each time we are faced with a weakness, we will learn to praise Him for His grace and say (as Paul does in the next verse), "When I am weak, I am strong!"

The kingdom of God often seems upside-down to us. The Bible tells us that in God's kingdom the poor are rich, the humble are exalted, and now we see another upside-down thought: the weak are strong. "When I am weak, I am strong." For the past 20 years I have been learning more and more about the freedom that comes when I truly understand that statement. Another way of saying it is "I can't, but God can."

I know that you have heard about Alcoholics Anonymous' 12 steps, which have helped millions of people all over the world to draw closer to God so He could help them recover from alcoholism. But you might not know that the steps were written by a group of Christians who took 12-Step principles directly from Scripture. "I can't, but God can," is the short form of AA's first two steps. In order for the miracle of recovery to happen in their lives, and in ours, we must first admit that without God's grace we are powerless over our weaknesses. Then immediately we can say with confidence: "I can't, but because of God's grace, He can help me to do anything He calls me to do."

Write About It

It wasn't until I quit falling into shame over my weaknesses and turned to God for help that I have been able to overcome them. I had to quit beating myself up for being weak and start praising the Lord for His strength at work in me. Do you beat yourself up over any weaknesses? List them here:

1. _____

2. _____

3. _____

4. _____

Pray About It

Now go from worry to worship by admitting your weaknesses to God and praising Him for the grace He is giving you to overcome them. Ask Him to help you to rely on His grace the next time you are faced with those weaknesses.

_____

_____

_____

_____

Reflect on Today's Verse as you journey from worry to worship. 2 Corinthians 12:9 *"My grace is sufficient for you, for my power is made perfect in weakness."*

Lord, thank You for Your grace—Your unmerited favor of me and unlimited power in me. Thank You that Your grace is always sufficient for me. Because of Your grace, I can stop beating myself up. You love me just the way I am, and Your power is at work in me, helping me to become the person I have always wanted to be.

No matter what mistakes I make, You will never stop loving me. No matter how many weaknesses I have, You will provide more than enough grace to turn each of my weaknesses into strengths when I rely on Your help. Thank You that nothing is too hard for You. Help me to begin living in a new way—to have an "I-can't-but-God-can" lifestyle so that I can quit focusing on my weaknesses and praise You for Your amazing grace instead.

Do It

Next time you are faced with a weakness say, "I can't, but God can!"

Chapter 3

God's Plan

Day 11

God knows what He is doing.

Today's Verse

Isaiah 40:13 — *"Who has understood the mind of the Lord, or instructed him as his counselor?"*

Read About It

Many people don't like God's plan for their lives. They would never say it, but they secretly believe that God is a killjoy, wanting to squelch their fun. They make the same mistake with their Heavenly Father that I almost made as a teenager with my dad. Let me tell you about it.

Larry was gorgeous. I was 15 and he was an "older man" of 18. How excited I was that he liked me. He was so cool. He dressed in jeans and a white tee shirt with the sleeves rolled up. My Fonzie look-alike had a ducktail haircut that was long and really stylish, especially with the faster, cooler crowd. I wasn't part of that group, but Larry liked me anyway. He asked me to go steady on our first date and I thought I had finally arrived because he wanted me to be his girlfriend.

My father's eyes widened when I introduced him to Larry that night, and his pupils constricted as they zoomed in on the cigarette casually dangling from Larry's lips. My father was usually so busy he didn't notice what I did or whom I dated, but he definitely noticed Larry.

Ten seconds after the door closed and Larry and I had said our goodnights, my dad said, "You're never going to date that hood again!" Instantly I thought: "Oh, yes I am," but fear kept me from saying it. He was my father after all. So, after many tears and much regret, I hesitantly told Larry that I couldn't see him again.

Three months later Larry and his new girlfriend came down with mononucleosis and were out of school the rest of the year. My father did know best, and I'm glad I listened to him.

Think About It

God has a plan for His children's lives, just as our parents had plans for us. He reveals it to us in the Bible. Colossians 2:6–7 gives us a good example of God's plan for each of us.

Colossians 2:6a (TLB) *"And now just as you trusted Christ to save you, trust him, too, for each day's problems."* God wants us to trust Him to save us from hell when we die and from a hell on earth that comes when we worry. Sometimes it is easier to trust God to handle the big problems than the smaller ones. A car that won't run, a snide remark, or a backache all seem to be too trivial to take to God. But He wants us to come to Him with all of our worries.

Colossians 2:6b (TLB) *"Live in vital union with him."* We live in vital union with God by remembering He is with us, relying on His power, and following the plan that He has for our lives. His plan is the same that almost all parents have for their children: that we love and obey Him, spend time with Him, and appreciate all that He is doing for us.

Colossians 2:7a (TLB) *"Let your roots grow down into him and draw up nourishment from him."* God wants us to be rooted and established in His love, not in things of the world. He wants to nourish us through His Word and His Spirit as well as the daily bread He provides for us.

Colossians 2:7b (TLB) *"See that you go on growing in the Lord."* God's plan for our lives is that we see to it that we go on growing in the Lord—to put spiritual growth first. Things that get in the way of that can even be things that seem good, like doing good deeds; but when they get in the way of growing in the Lord, they are not in God's plan for us.

Colossians 2:7c (TLB) *"Become strong and vigorous in the truth you were taught."* God wants us to practice the principles He teaches us in His Word. For example, the way He teaches us to be patient is to allow things to come into our lives that will give us opportunities to practice patience. There is no other way to build up our spiritual muscles than to practice doing what God tells us to do one day at a time.

Colossians 2:7d (TLB) *"Let your lives overflow with joy and thanksgiving for all he has done."* God wants us to praise Him for all His good works in our lives. When we live this lifestyle of praise, we overflow with joy and we go from worry to worship.

Write About It

In order to cooperate with the plan that God has for your life, answer the following questions and see which area needs most attention. Pray and ask God to help you to choose one or two of the corresponding practical tips to help you in that area.

Colossians 2:6a (TLB) *"And now just as you trusted Christ to save you, trust him, too, for each day's problems."*

Yes___ No___ 1. Do you spend a few minutes every morning with the Lord preparing for your day?

Yes___ No___ 2. Do you usually remember to pray when you are faced by a problem during the day?

Practical Tip: Each morning, list the problems you will be facing that day and pray about them. Then pray again when confronted with the problem during the day.

Colossians 2:6b (TLB) *"Live in vital union with him."*

Yes___ No___ 3. When fretting about something, do you remember God is there to help you?

Practical Tip: When making a decision, stop for a moment to consult the Lord. If you know what Jesus would do, pray for the willingness and ability to do it.

Colossians 2:7a (TLB) *"Let your roots grow down into him and draw up nourishment from him."*

Yes___ No___ 4. When you're upset, do you reach for food or something else to calm you down?

Practical Tip: Spend time daily memorizing Scripture. Keep a list of all of the passages you've memorized and brush up on them often. Nothing will keep you more rooted in the Lord!

Colossians 2:7b (TLB) *"See that you go on growing in the Lord."*

Yes___ No___ 5. Even during busy times, do you do things every day that will help you to grow in the Lord so you won't wither spiritually?

Practical Tip: Make an achievable goal that will help you to grow spiritually; for example, go to church each Sunday, have a 15-minute quiet time daily, memorize Scripture for three minutes a day, or join a Bible study class.

Colossians 2:7c (TLB) *"Become strong and vigorous in the truth you were taught."*

Yes___ No___ 6. Do you follow God's leading even when He's asking you to do something challenging?

Practical Tip: Make a list of things that God is leading you to do, and pray for willingness to do them.

Colossians 2:7d (TLB) *"Let your lives overflow with joy and thanksgiving for all he has done."*

Yes___ No___ 7. Do you spend a few minutes every day thanking God for your blessings?

Practical Tip: Try using the ACTS format for your prayers— ACTS stands for Adoration, Confession, Thanksgiving, Supplication. This format will help you remember daily to praise God, confess your sins, thank God for blessings, and ask God for specific things for yourself and others.

Pray About It 🙏

Write a prayer confessing any *no* answers on the question-naire at left, which revealed areas that need changing. Pray for help in making these changes.

_____

_____

_____

_____

Reflect on Today's Verse as you journey from worry to worship. Isaiah 40:13 *"Who has understood the mind of the Lord, or instructed him as his counselor?"*

Father, I confess that many times I have refused to follow Your plan for my life. I have acted like a disrespectful teenager, telling You what to do rather than letting You direct me. I have questioned You when things happened to me that I didn't understand. I have been disappointed in You and pouted when I didn't get my own way. I have made excuses so I could do my own thing. I have disobeyed You and pretended that You wouldn't know. Father, I come humbly to You now asking You to forgive me. Help me to follow the plan you have for my life and to spend my days praising You for it.

Do It

Have a daily quiet time. It's the most productive time you will ever spend.

Day 12
God knows what He is doing.

Today's Verse

Jeremiah 29:11 *"For I know the plans I have for you," declares the Lord, "plans to prosper you and not to harm you, plans to give you hope and a future."*

Read About It

My friend Mary and I were talking last week about why she was so worried. She said, "I feel like I'm living in a state of limbo. I don't know how my life will turn out. My kids are rebelling, my husband doesn't have a job, and my blood pressure is out of sight. I can't stop worrying until I know that all of these things will be okay."

I thought about Mary's words and I can understand why she

hates "living in limbo." The suspense is killing her. I don't like being in suspense either. That's the reason I always enjoy watching a movie better the second time. That way I know how the movie will end; and even if it's sad, at least I'm prepared for it and I don't have to wonder what will happen.

Mary interrupted my thoughts to ask, "Wouldn't it be nice if we didn't have to live in suspense—if we could know God's plan for our lives now, rather than having to wait to see it unfold later?"

Her question gave me something to think about, and I answered it thoughtfully, "We can know God's plan for our lives without having to wait another minute. He tells us in Jeremiah 29:11 that He has plans to prosper us and not harm us. We can rest assured that whatever plans He has for us are good, even if we don't know the details of what they are. We don't have to worry about the future because our future is in good hands."

Think About It

Let's review some of the things we have talked about so far to help the truth of Jeremiah 29:11 sink in.

- In the first week we talked about God's omnipresence— God is with each one of us at all times. He never leaves us and is constantly watching over us. He is there to help us to walk in the plan He has for us.
- In the second week we studied God's omnipotence—God has unlimited power. He has the power to keep us from anything that would ultimately be harmful to us.
- Yesterday we talked about God's omniscience—God has unlimited understanding and knowledge. He sees the future and He knows the best plan for our lives.
- Next week we will talk about God's purpose. We will explore reasons why God allows us to experience difficult circumstances and be reassured that He has purpose for all of our pain.

We are learning how to put these and other biblical concepts together as building blocks to form a firm foundation of faith so we can go from worry to worship.

Write About It ✐

> Yes___ No___ Do you really believe what God says in today's verse—that He has plans to prosper you and not to harm you?

Do you remember the story in Mark 9:24 about the father of the sick child who was having problems believing that Jesus really would help him? The father said, "I do believe; help me overcome my unbelief!" How did Jesus respond to him?

_____

_____

_____

Was He irritated because of the man's incomplete faith? Did He give the father a lecture? Jesus responded with compassion by immediately healing the sick child. That is the way Jesus is responding to you today. Jesus loves you. He gave His life for you. He is not rejecting you because of your worries. He feels compassion for you and wants to help you to have faith.

Pray About It 🙏

Ask God to give you faith to believe fully that Jeremiah 29:11 is true for you personally.

_____

_____

_____

_____

Reflect on Today's Verse as you journey from worry to worship. Jeremiah 29:11 *"For I know the plans I have for you,"* *declares the Lord, "plans to prosper you and not to harm you,* *plans to give you hope and a future."*

Lord, thank You for the plans You have for me. Thank You for *reassuring me that Your plans are to prosper me and not harm* *me. I guess my idea of prosperity has been comfort and ease,* *and Your idea of prosperity is much deeper than that. You* *want our relationship to grow in intimacy, and my life to have* *meaning. I want that too. I put my life in Your hands and I* *trust You to work out Your plans for me.*

Do It

When you have doubts, say, "Lord, I believe; help me overcome my unbelief!"

Day 13

God knows what He is doing.

Today's Verse

Ephesians 2:10 *"We are God's workmanship,* *created in Christ Jesus to do good works, which* *God prepared in advance for us to do."*

Read About It

According to today's verse, we are God's workmanship, created in Christ Jesus. God has a plan for each of our lives, which He decided on before we were even born. But many people are so busy worrying about things that are not of lasting importance that they don't make time to do what God has called them to do. These people will not find lasting peace until they start living more in God's plan— "in Christ Jesus." Let's see what the Bible has to say about the benefits of living in Christ. Here are a few of the 89 references I found.

Promise for those living in Christ	Scripture
We don't experience hell when we die.	**Romans 6:23**— "For the wages of sin is death, but the gift of God is eternal life *in Christ Jesus* our Lord."
We don't have to experience hell on earth while we live.	**Philippians 4:7**— "And the peace of God, which transcends all understanding, will guard your hearts and your minds *in Christ Jesus.*"
We don't have to fear death or judgment.	**Romans 8:1–2**— "Therefore, there is now no condemnation for those who are in Christ Jesus, because through *Christ Jesus* the law of the Spirit of life set me free from the law of sin and death."
We can be close to God.	**Ephesians 2:13**— "But now in *Christ Jesus* you who once were far away have been brought near through the blood of Christ."
We can be freed from our past.	**2 Corinthians 5:17**— "Therefore, if anyone is *in Christ*, he is a new creation; the old has gone, the new has come!"
We have everything that we need.	**Philippians 4:19**— "And my God will meet all your needs according to his glorious riches *in Christ Jesus.*

Since the beginning of this book, we have been talking about living in Christ Jesus—having a close personal relationship with the Living God who is a work in us. This intimacy with God through Christ is God's plan for our lives. Here are some of the word pictures we have talked about that describe this relationship:

• He is a Shepherd tending to us, and we are His flock (Isaiah 40:11)
• He is our Counselor (John 14:26)
• We are His children (John 1:12)
• We are His beloved, resting secure between His shoulders (Deuteronomy 33:12)
• He sings love songs over us (Zephaniah 3:17)
• He takes hold of our hands and says He will help us (Isaiah 41:13)
• He tells us to yoke ourselves to Him so we can find rest (Matthew 11:28)
• He feels compassion toward us like a nursing mother feels toward her baby (Isaiah 49:15)
• He is the vine and we are the branches; without Him we can do nothing (John 15:5)
• His grace is a gift He gives us (Ephesians 2:8–9)
• Our roots grow down into Him and draw up nourishment from Him (Colossians 2:7)

Anything we do that gets in the way of this close relationship is not God's plan for our lives.

Think About It

**Here is a one-question quiz.
Test yourself to see if you understand
what living in Christ means.**

1. God's plan is that you live "in Christ Jesus." What
   does that mean?

   _____

   _____

   _____

   _____

Answer: Living in Christ Jesus means that I will have a close
personal relationship with the Living God, who is at work in
me—that I have intimacy with God through Christ Jesus.

Now answer these questions.

1. With what person do you have your closest relationship?

   _____

2. What do you do to keep this relationship close?

   _____

   _____

   _____

   _____

3. Do you do these things to *make* the person love you?

   _____

4. What would happen if you were always too busy to do any
of these things with or for this person?

   _____

5. How would this person feel if you offered to pay so that he

or she would love you?

_____

6. If this person wrote letters to you, what would happen if you didn't make time to read them?

_____

7. How would this person feel if every time he or she asked to spend time with you, you always said that you were too busy doing something else?

_____

Let me share my answers with you about the person with whom I have my closest relationship—my husband.

To Keep Our Relationship Close I Do Several Things
- Make time for him and think about him a lot.
- Have meaningful conversations, which include both of us listening, speaking, and saying nice things to each other.
- Care about things that are important to him.
- Do nice things for him, not to make him love me, but to demonstrate my love.
- If my husband asks me not to do something, I make an effort not to do it to demonstrate my love.
- If my husband asks me to do something, I make an effort to do it to show him how much I love him.

My husband and I spend a lot of time sitting together on our deck overlooking the woods in our backyard. Our relationship would suffer terribly if every time my husband asked me to come and sit next to him, I answered, "I'm too busy, but you can tag along with me while I do something else." It is fine to talk to him while I am doing something else, but we need to spend time together daily just enjoying each other's company and sharing our thoughts and feelings.

It is the same with my relationship with God.

As I go through each day, I spend time talking to God, thinking about Him, and doing things to please Him. I pray while I am driving, doing housework, or weeding my garden, but it's also important for us to spend time together every day without any distractions. **That is why I have daily quiet times.** It amazes me how these few minutes spent together every day bring intimacy and freshness to our relationship.

Write About It ✐

What is God encouraging you to do to have a closer relationship with Him?

_____

_____

_____

_____

When you have a close relationship with God, you will experience His love and will want to share it with others. As you spend time with Him every day in prayer and Bible study, He will show you good works He wants you to do. And He will give you the desire and ability to do them.

Pray About It 🙏

Reflect on today's verse as you journey from worry to worship. Ephesians 2:10 *"We are God's workmanship, created in Christ Jesus to do good works, which God prepared in advance for us to do."*

Reread the promises for those who are "in Christ." Thank God that those promises are a reality in your life, and pray that He will lead you to do the works He has prepared for you to do.

_____

_____

_____

_____

Lord, thank You that Jesus is my Savior so I am in Christ. Help me to never take this privilege for granted. Show me, Lord, how to draw closer to You and do the works You prepared in advance for me to do. I praise You that I don't have to do anything to earn Your love because You already love me perfectly—just as I am. And I praise You for equipping me to do good works so I can share Your love with others.

Do It 👣

If you ever say that you are too busy to pray, slow down because you are too busy.

_____

Day 14
God knows what He is doing.

Today's Verse

Proverbs 23:25–26 *"Have no fear of sudden disaster or of the ruin that overtakes the wicked, for the Lord will be your confidence and will keep your foot from being snared."*

Read About It

Two years ago my sister Linda was in a devastating auto accident. She was in a coma for almost a month, swaying precariously between life and death. When she woke up from the coma, Linda's mind was sound, but she was unable to walk or talk so she could be easily understood. And she had such a terrible tremor from the brain damage that she could hardly feed herself.

How could this be God's plan for this precious Christian? Her accident seemed like a sudden disaster that would result in meaningless suffering for the rest of her life. But Linda did not think so.

After months in a hospital and nursing home, Linda was released to an assisted-living facility. She knew God had a plan and she was determined to cooperate with Him. Linda continued to work hard learning how to maneuver her wheelchair so she could get about on her own. She worked on her speech for hours at a time. The tremor got progressively worse, so everyone thought she would have to give up her two favorite post-accident activities—writing her prayers and Bible meditations. But not being able to write didn't slow Linda down. She started typing. How amazing it is to see her joyfully pecking away at her typewriter with one or two very shaky fingers.

Linda has never lost her smile, and her smile speaks more eloquently about the Lord than anyone ever could with words. Even though she can't talk as clearly as before, everyone marvels at the positive influence she is on those around her, and at the joy and contentment she feels most of the time. Linda seldom complains and always has an encouraging word to say. And God is using her in mighty ways.

Linda has confidence that the Lord has a plan for her. At this time in her life, God's plan is not to use her brilliant mind or her PhD in clinical psychology. It is to use her smile to reflect His love to people who need to know He cares.

Think About It

This week we are talking about God's plan. Yesterday we said that His plan is for us to live in Christ and do the good works that God prepared in advance for us to do. Sometimes, as in Linda's case, the good works that God has prepared are not ones that we would choose or expect. But we can rest in the knowledge that when we are doing whatever God has called us to do, we can experience joy and find contentment, no matter the circumstances.

Paul knew that. Listen to his words, written from prison awaiting his execution: Philippians 4:11–13 *"I have learned to be content whatever the circumstances. I know what it is to be in need, and I know what it is to have plenty. I have learned the secret of being content in any and every situation, whether well fed or hungry, whether living in plenty or in want. I can do everything through him who gives me strength."*

Paul had confidence in the Lord. He didn't fear sudden disaster or ruin because he knew this very important fact: **God has a plan for each of our lives—to profit us and not harm us. His plan is to make our lives meaningful and productive, to allow us to experience His joy and contentment as we reflect His love to a hurting world, and when we are done, to take us home to heaven.**

Paul understood that God's plan included even his imprisonment, but he might not have realized why. If Paul had not been in prison, he might not have written many of the letters of the New Testament. Paul didn't know exactly what God was doing, but he still didn't worry about what would happen because he knew that his future was in good hands.

Abraham is another example of someone who had confidence in God's plan, even though he didn't know how God would work it out. In Hebrews 11:8 God commends Abraham because of his faith. When God told him to go to a new place, he "obeyed and went, even though he did not know where he was going."

**God said to Abraham, "Come with me. I'll tell you
where we're going when we get there!"
Is God telling you the same thing?**

Write About It ✎

1. Are you willing to go where the Lord leads you, even
though you don't know where you are going? If so, tell the
Lord about your willingness to follow Him.

_____

_____

_____

_____

2. Are you holding back because you fear sudden disaster or
ruin? **If so, your foot is snared because of a lack of confidence in the Lord's plan for your life.** Describe what happens when someone's foot is snared (caught in a trap). How
has the snare interfered with your life?

_____

_____

_____

_____

Pray About It 🙏

Reflect on Today's Verse as you journey from worry to worship. Proverbs 23:25–26 *"Have no fear of sudden disaster or of
the ruin that overtakes the wicked, for the Lord will be your
confidence and will keep your foot from being snared."*

List the specific things you have been worrying about. Ask
the Lord to give you more confidence in His plan concerning
these things.

_____

_____

_____

_____

Lord, thank You that I don't have to worry, cross my fingers, or hope for good luck. I can live in confidence, knowing that my future is in good hands. When I experience trials, my trials will have purpose, and they will not overwhelm me. You have a purpose for any pain I experience. When I have confidence in You, I can find joy and contentment in the midst of every situation.

Do It

Rest in the knowledge that you will be able to find joy and contentment no matter what happens.

Day 15
God knows what He is doing.

Today's Verse

1 John 4:18 *(TLB) "We need have no fear of someone who loves us perfectly; his perfect love for us eliminates all dread of what he might do to us. If we are afraid, it is for fear of what he might do to us, and shows that we are not fully convinced that he really loves us."*

Read About It

Susan, an attractive woman of 35, came to me for counseling because she had been having panic attacks. As soon as I asked how I could help her, she blurted out what was on her mind. "A loving God would never allow bad things to happen to good people. I am a good Christian. I pray, go to church, and study the Bible, yet I don't have enough money to pay my bills."

She continued without stopping to take a breath, "Either God can't help or He is refusing to. How can I trust Him if He won't bless me even though I am doing everything I can to be a good Christian?"

Susan was really mad. She denied it, of course, but her anger was eating her alive. She was mad at God because He had let her down. He didn't meet any of her expectations of how a loving God should treat His children. And He was withholding blessings she felt entitled to.

She ended her accusations by spewing out this question, "How could God be so unfair?"

Susan and I had a lot of work to do, but I saw right away what Susan's problem was: she was basing her understanding of God on misconceptions. Here are some of them and a corresponding truth from the Bible.

"I am a good person, entitled to blessings from God."

Psalm 130:3–4— "If you, O Lord, kept a record of sins, O Lord, who could stand? But with you there is forgiveness."

Susan had a sense of entitlement because she was a "good" person. The truth is that, apart from God's grace through Christ, she deserved only His wrath.

"I am a 'good' Christian because I go to church, pray, and read the Bible."

Psalm 51:17 (NLT) "The sacrifice you want is a broken spirit. A broken and repentant heart, O God, you will not despise."

Susan was proud of herself for keeping some of God's commands, but God detests our pride. He doesn't want a few minutes of our day; He wants us to have a new heart, full of love and repentance.

"I expect God to do what I want because I do some of the things He wants."

Matthew 26:39 (KJV)— *"And he went a little further, and fell on his face, and prayed, saying, O my Father, if it be possible, let this cup pass from me: nevertheless, not as I will, but as thou wilt."*

Susan had a demanding attitude toward God, but God wants us to have a "nevertheless attitude." Jesus models this attitude for us. When facing the cross, Jesus tells God His desires, and then says, "Nevertheless, not as I will . . . ."

"I know more than God about what is best."

Romans 9:20— *"But who are you, O man, to talk back to God? Shall what is formed say to him who formed it, 'Why did you make me like this?'"*

When we make demands of God and get mad that He isn't doing what we tell Him to do, we are putting ourselves above God and making a mockery of Him.

"God is unfair."

Psalm 89:14 (NLT)— *"Your throne is founded on two strong pillars—righteousness and justice."*

Susan was sitting in judgment of God—not a wise thing to do.

"Hardship is always bad."

Hebrews 12:7 (NLT)— *"As you endure this divine discipline, remember that God is treating you as his own children. Whoever heard of a child who was never disciplined?"*

Susan had been acting like a spoiled child, upset because she didn't get her way. We talked about this in our counseling sessions, and she eventually prayed asking God to forgive her for doubting His love and to help her want His will. Not too much later, her panic attacks stopped. Eventually Susan got a new job and her financial situation improved. But she says that she often looks back on that difficult time and the valuable lesson she needed to learn: "My Heavenly Father knows best," she declares happily.

Think About It

What a precious Father we have! He loves us perfectly.

• He is omniscient; He has unlimited wisdom so He knows what is best for us.

• He is omnipotent; He has unlimited power so He can provide what is best for us.

• He is omnipresent; He is everywhere at the same time so He can watch over each one of us at all times.

• He is immutable; He never changes. He is faithful, consistent, and unswerving in His dedication to us.

• He is gracious; He freely gives favor and power to those who have faith in His Son.

• He is compassionate; He sympathizes with us, takes pity on us, and is concerned about us.

• He sacrificed His only Son to save us. There is no greater love than this.

Write About It

Yes___ No___   1. Do you tend to get your feelings hurt when God doesn't bless you like you want?

Yes___ No___   2. Do you say, "God is good" when good things happen and secretly believe the opposite when bad things happen?

Yes___ No___   3. When bad things happen to "good" people, do you believe that God is unfair?

Yes___ No___   4. Do you sometimes believe that your plan is better than God's?

5. Yes___ No___Do you do good things expecting God to pay
you back by giving you what you want?
6. Yes___ No___Do you believe that you deserve the blessings
God gives you?

If you had any *yes* answers, write about them here. It would also be a good idea to talk them over with a respected Christian friend, pastor, or Christian counselor.

_____

_____

_____

Pray About It

There is a big difference between having a belligerent attitude toward God and expressing heartfelt grief to Him. But no matter what we are feeling, we need to tell God about it. Read Psalm 13, David's prayer in which he pours out his hurts to God. David starts out telling God his worries and ends up going from worry to worship.

Psalm 13

How long, O Lord? Will you forget me forever?
How long will you hide your face from me?
How long must I wrestle with my thoughts
and every day have sorrow in my heart?
How long will my enemy triumph over me?
Look on me and answer, O Lord my God.
Give light to my eyes, or I will sleep in death;
my enemy will say, "I have overcome him,"
and my foes will rejoice when I fall.
But I trust in your unfailing love;
my heart rejoices in your salvation.
I will sing to the Lord,
for he has been good to me.

If you feel that God has been unfair to you or you don't understand His plan, pour out your hurts to Him. Ask Him to help you to trust that He loves you perfectly. Continue this on another page if needed. Know that God wants you to express your feelings and if you share your hurts with Him, He will help you to let go of them.

_____

_____

_____

_____

_____

Reflect on today's verse as you journey from worry to worship. 1 John 4:18 (TLB) *"We need have no fear of someone who loves us perfectly; his perfect love for us eliminates all dread of what he might do to us. If we are afraid, it is for fear of what he might do to us, and shows that we are not fully convinced that he really loves us."*

Lord, in this verse You say, "We need have no fear." That means that worry is a choice, so instead of worrying, I will choose today to do these two things: I will stop complaining and start praising You for Your perfect love. If my worry returns, I will know that I have started looking at my problems instead of Your promises, so I will start praising You again and turn my worry back to worship.

Do It

If your worship turns to worry, get back to work and reverse the process.

Chapter 4

God's Purpose

Day 16

No pain is wasted in God's economy.

Today's Verse

Isaiah 40:5 *"And the glory of the Lord will be revealed, and all mankind together will see it."*

Read About It

We often have to endure pain that seems like wasted torture inflicted on us, but God always has a purpose for any pain He allows to come into our lives, even if we can't see it at the time. When we trust God to use our pain for our good and His glory, we can turn our worries to worship. Let me tell you about an incident that helped me to learn that.

My three-year-old daughter Sarah was playing one summer afternoon with her friend Christy when Christy dropped a board on Sarah's little toe. Terrified by Sarah's shrieks and her swollen purple toe, I quickly gathered her up and rushed to the emergency room. The doctor had to remove the toenail and suture a tiny artery that had ruptured. Though he used a local anesthetic, it didn't deaden the pain.

As I held Sarah down on the stretcher trying to reassure her while the doctor worked, she looked up at me and sobbed, "Mommy, why are you letting him hurt me?" My tears mingled with hers and I held her close as I said, "Precious one, the pain is necessary and it hurts me too."

Years later, while dealing with pain caused by a verbally-abusive father, I asked God why He allowed me to be hurt so deeply. In an instant, the picture of my daughter in the emergency room flooded my mind and I remembered the words I said, but this time God was saying them to me: "Precious one, the pain was necessary and it hurt Me too."

At that moment I finally understood that God suffered with me while I trembled at the feet of my angry father. And I realized that, just as Sarah's pain had a purpose, mine did too.

Without the pain of my childhood, God's glory would not have been revealed in me as fully. I wouldn't have learned to rely on Him to help me overcome my hurts. And I wouldn't have written books and presented seminars around the country telling other hurting people about God's power to help them. God had a purpose for my pain and I praise Him for it.

Think About It

In the Bible God explains why He allows adversity into our lives. Here are some of the reasons He gives:

Because of adversity I will seek God. Hosea 5:15— "In their misery they will earnestly seek me."

Because of adversity I will be able to help others more effectively. 2 Corinthians 1:3–4— "The Father of compassion and the God of all comfort, who comforts us in all our troubles, so that we can comfort those in any trouble with the comfort we ourselves have received from God."

Because of adversity I can experience God's power at work in my life. 2 Corinthians 12:9–10— "[God said] 'My grace is sufficient for you, for my power is made perfect in weakness.' Therefore I will boast all the more gladly about my weaknesses, so that Christ's power may rest on me. That is why, for Christ's sake, I delight in weaknesses, in insults, in hardships, in persecutions, in difficulties. For when I am weak, then I am strong."

Because of adversity I can grow up in my faith and be a more mature believer. James 1:2–4— "Consider it pure joy, my brothers, whenever you face trials of many kinds, because you know that the testing of your faith develops perseverance. Perseverance must finish its work so that you may be mature and complete, not lacking anything."

Because of adversity I won't be like a spoiled child. Hebrews 12:10— "Our fathers disciplined us for a little while as they thought best; but God disciplines us for our good, that we may share in his holiness."

Because of adversity I can learn to trust God's protection. Psalm 18:2— "The Lord is my rock, my fortress and my deliverer; my God is my rock, in whom I take refuge. He is my shield and the horn of my salvation, my stronghold."

Because of adversity I can experience deep fellowship. 2 Corinthians 1:7— "We know that just as you share in our sufferings, so also you share in our comfort."

Because of adversity I can experience deeper intimacy with the Lord. Psalm 34:18— "The Lord is close to the brokenhearted and saves those who are crushed in spirit."

Because of adversity God can be glorified in me. John 9:1–3— "As he went along, he saw a man blind from birth. His

disciples asked him, 'Rabbi, who sinned, this man or his parents, that he was born blind?' 'Neither this man nor his parents
sinned,' said Jesus, 'but this happened so that the work of God
might be displayed in his life.'"

Write About It

Make a list, on another sheet of paper or in your prayer notebook, of hurts you have experienced and how God has used
them. If God hasn't used them yet, imagine how God may use
your hurts someday.

Pray About It

Write your prayer thanking God for using your pain for your
good and His glory.

_____

_____

_____

_____

Reflect on today's verse as you journey from worry to worship. Isaiah 40:5 *"And the glory of the Lord will be revealed,
and all mankind together will see it."*

*Lord, thank You that Your glory is being revealed in me, not in
spite of my worries, but because of them. Now that I know that
You don't allow painful things to come into my life without a
reason, I have stopped asking, "Why me, Lord?" Instead, I ask,
"What would You have me learn?" or "How will You use my
pain to help others?" When I focus on You I am able to turn my
worries to worship and Your glory is revealed in me once more.*

Do It

Next time you find yourself saying, "Why me?" ask God instead, "What would You have me learn?" or "How are You going to use this pain?"

Day 17

No pain is wasted in God's economy.

Today's Verse

James 1:2–4 *"Consider it pure joy, my brothers, whenever you face trials of many kinds, because you know that the testing of your faith develops perseverance. Perseverance must finish its work so that you may be mature and complete, not lacking anything."*

Read About It

I grew up living in the "if onlys." Whenever I faced a problem that would not go away, I didn't try to overcome it; I just said, "if only" over it. Let me explain.

My father was a rageaholic. I never knew when he was going to explode and worried constantly that I would set him off. I was sure that I could never be happy living with him, and as long as I can remember, I dreamed of how perfect life would be away from my father. This simple phrase started my "if-only" way of coping with trials. "If only I could get away from my dad, I would be happy."

I found that overeating helped calm me, but as my body grew, my worries grew with them. All the kids made fun of me because of my weight. I coped by telling myself, "If only I weren't fat, I would be happy."

I had a skinny sister. To make matters worse, she was smart, too. She could study for just a few minutes and get almost all As. But I made horrible grades. I tried to study but I wasn't able to concentrate, so I would sneak down to the kitchen to get a little something "to help me think." After eating, I would do a lot of thinking. I would think about how lucky my sister was, how awful my life was, how stupid I was and, of course, I would think, "If only I were smart, I would be happy."

My list of "if onlys" went on and on. But when I went away to college, all of my "if onlys" happened.

Dad wasn't around, so I didn't have to worry about him, but I still wasn't happy. I started making good grades when I learned how to study and stopped telling myself I couldn't do it, but that didn't make me happy. And I finally got thin. I went on a strict diet—mainly existing on occasional candy bars and cheese crackers from the machine in the dorm. I was thin, but even that didn't make me happy.

I was sure marriage would finally make me happy, and I married my college sweetheart. Even though I had a precious husband, something was missing and I still wasn't happy. I said to myself, "If only I had a baby, I would be happy." But after little Michael was born, I still wasn't happy. So I did what so many mothers do; I said, "If only I had a job, I would be happy." Soon I began teaching Spanish in high school.

Dealing with 100 teenagers, a much-neglected husband, and shuffling my son to day care didn't make me happy. By November of that year, my blood pressure shot up to a dangerous level. The medication wasn't helping much and I knew that my unhappiness was contributing to the problem, but I didn't know what I could do about it.

One afternoon on a routine visit to check on my blood pressure, Dr. Jones invited me to join a group he was starting, "to help you deal with your problems better," he said. It was in that group that I confessed Jesus as my Savior and I finally got free of my "if onlys."

Without my high blood pressure, I might still be stuck in the "if onlys" and without Christ. That trial was the best thing that could have happened to me. It made me let go of my old way of coping and reach out to the Lord. He helped me to realize that I was wasting my life dreaming of the day when all of my circumstances would be just the way I wanted them.

While stuck in my if-only way of living, I couldn't grow in maturity or understanding. I couldn't learn to persevere in overcoming obstacles or make the most of what I had. Instead, I wasted my days waiting for a happily-ever-after that didn't exist. I am very thankful for my high blood pressure. I certainly wasn't at the time, but now I can consider that trial "pure joy." Because of it, I found something better than the happiness I was searching for. I found a lasting joy and completeness in Christ, which is far better.

Think About It

You have probably found, as I did, that life is filled with problems, and as soon as one problem is solved, there are many others to take its place. There will never be a perfect time when you have everything you want.

Don't do like I did and waste your time searching for a magical happily-ever-after, saying, "if only this would happen . . ." or "if only that would go away, I would be happy." Happiness is never permanent because it depends on circumstances, and circumstances can change in an instant. Happiness is hard to find and impossible to keep. Many spend entire lifetimes searching for it and worrying about not finding it.

Joy, on the other hand, does not depend on circumstances. It is a fruit of the Spirit, which comes as a result of having a close relationship with Christ. We can experience joy in all situations. It bubbles up inside of us as we praise God for what

He is doing in our lives. Joy grows as we calmly accept the things in life that we cannot change and change the things with God's help that we can change. Amazingly, the deepest joy often comes during trials. But as long as we live in the "if onlys" we will not experience it.

Write About It

Are you living in the "if onlys"? Take this little quiz to find out. Place a check next to any of the following things you have told yourself. Add any additional "if onlys" that come to mind:

❑ If only my loved one were a Christian, I would be happy.
❑ If only I had enough money, I would be happy.
❑ If only I got married (divorced, had children, etc.), I would be happy.
❑ If only I had better health, I would be happy.
❑ If only I didn't have to work so hard, I would be happy.
❑ If only there wasn't a danger of war and terrorism, I would be happy.
❑ If only my loved one(s) made better choices, I would be happy.
❑ If only my mate (boss, mother, child, etc.) would change, I would be happy.
❑ If only_____, I would be happy.
❑ If only_____, I would be happy.
❑ If only_____, I would be happy.
❑ If only_____, I would be happy.

Even if you just had one check, you have a problem with the "if onlys." In order to journey from worry to worship, it is important to let go of this type of thinking.

Get rid of your "if onlys"!

Finish this sentence as it relates to your most significant "if only":

I feel that I won't be happy or content until

_____.

In order to get rid of your "if onlys," transform your thoughts.

• Read the following each time you start to say, "if only."

Thought Transformer

God's Word says that I can be content in any and every situation (Philippians 4:12). I choose to believe His truth. Therefore, I will change my way of thinking. Instead of "if only," I will say this: It would be wonderful if what I want so badly happened. I would love it if

_____,

_____,

_____,

but this does not affect my joy. I can be joyful even if this problem never changes. Today I choose to stop worrying about what I am lacking. Instead, I praise God for His presence with me, His power at work in and around me, His plan for my life, and His purpose for this pain I am experiencing. I choose to focus on the Lord and know that He will help me to turn my worries to worship.

Pray About It

Reflect on today's verse as you journey from worry to worship. James 1:2–4 *"Consider it pure joy, my brothers, whenever you face trials of many kinds, because you know that the testing of your faith develops perseverance. Perseverance must finish its work so that you may be mature and complete, not lacking anything."*

Pray that God will help you to let go of your "if onlys" so you can take hold of His hand and let Him lead you to joy.

_____

_____

_____

_____

Lord, thank You for helping me to grow up in my faith. You allow trials of many kinds to test my faith and help me to look only to You for satisfaction. I determine today to quit saying "if only" and to stand firm against this kind of thinking. Instead of saying "if only," I will thank You, God, that You have a plan for my life and a purpose for me. I know that You will help me to become more mature, joyful and complete in Christ.

Do It

When experiencing trials, don't say, "if only . . ." Instead, praise God for His purpose and watch for joy to come!

Day 18

No pain is wasted in God's economy.

Today's Verse

2 Corinthians 1:9 *"Indeed, in our hearts we felt the sentence of death. But this happened that we might not rely on ourselves but on God, who raises the dead."*

Read About It

I'll never read this passage again without thinking about the day Valeria died in my Bible class.

Valeria was talking about Today's Verse, 2 Corinthians 1:9, minutes before her heart stopped beating. It happened suddenly, with no warning. Her daughter, sitting next to her, was the first to notice that something was wrong and then, when Valeria slumped over in her chair, it was obvious to the entire class.

I did CPR while everyone prayed and, by the time the paramedics arrived, Valeria had been raised from the dead and was praising the Lord for delivering her. She recovered fully, but for a while, her heart had stopped beating!

How odd that she would discuss a verse about a sentence of death just before her heart stopped beating. "One of life's little coincidences," some might say, but I don't think so. God often leaves His calling card out in plain sight, and this is one of those times.

I remember when I heard my own death sentence. I was gaining weight by the tons—or so it felt—and I couldn't stop eating. My heart was so overworked trying to take care of those extra pounds that my blood pressure went crazy. My doctor said if I didn't lose weight, I would have a stroke. That day was a turning point in my life—a wake-up call. I realized that I had to do something about my problem, and I finally became willing to do what it took to change.

Looking back, I know that this shocking word from my doctor was spoken so I would finally quit trying to rely myself— my non-existent willpower and fad diets. After my wake-up call I knew I had to learn how to rely on the Lord to help me with my eating.

Twenty years later I feel younger and I am thinner and healthier than I was then. Because of my weight problem and the shocking death sentence my doctor pronounced over me, I have learned the practical ways to rely on the Lord that I am sharing with you.

Think About It

Someone once said, "We won't know God is all we need until God is all we have." I am sure that is exactly where God wants us to be—at a place where we recognize that we can't fix our problems and He is our only hope. How can we build our faith and have total confidence in the Lord unless we face impossible situations—things that are beyond our strength or control?

Maybe you are at that place as you read this. If so, be glad.

One day I told a Christian friend about my problems (there were many at that point), and she said something that I didn't like at the time, but now her words make sense. She said, "Embrace the pain. It will help you to know God better and cling more tightly to Him."

Some waste days, months, and even a lifetime trying to escape their problems or numb the pain. But when we "embrace the pain" and the One who can deliver us from it, we recognize the purpose for our pain and learn the lessons God is trying to teach us.

"Embracing the pain" does not mean that we enjoy trials or seek them; it means that we face them and recognize that they come with a plan and a purpose. "Embracing the pain" doesn't mean that we quit trying to solve our problems or praying for a miracle; it means that we accept the things that we cannot change and change the things that we can by relying on the Lord.

When we embrace the pain instead of running from it, we can deal with our problems in the Lord's strength.

Write About It ✎

1. Do you want to learn how to do that? Start by making a list of the problems you are facing today. List everything you are worrying about, no matter how trivial. Continue on another page if needed.

2. Now go through the list and place a star next to each of the problems that you have no control over. NOTE: You need to remember this as you place your stars: in addition to the obvious things that you can't control, such as things that happened in the past, war, terrorism, the economy, certain illnesses, etc., you cannot change anyone else. All you do when you try is make them angry and yourself miserable.

3. Make a Miracle List. Place the worries that you have no control over on the Miracle List below and put a copy of it in
   your prayer notebook. Pray over this list daily and thank
   God that these are His worries now. You are giving them to
   Him since you can't do anything about them.

Miracle List

*Lord, I give these things to you. I have no control over them. My
responsibility is to pray, trust You with these things, and leave
them in your hands.*

1.

2.

3.

4.

5.

6.

7.

Pray About It

Reflect on today's verse as you journey from worry to worship. 2 Corinthians 1:9 *"Indeed, in our hearts we felt the sentence of death. But this happened that we might not rely on
ourselves but on God, who raises the dead."*

_____

_____

_____

_____

*Lord, there have been times when I have felt that I could no
longer continue to endure all my problems. My worries seemed
overwhelming to me, and I tried to run from the pain. But I
bring my problems to You now and trust that You will help me*

to deal with each on of them. *You can do mighty miracles that would be impossible for me. So I relax my grip on my problems and ask You to take care of them for me—the things I can't change and the things that I can change with Your help. Help me to quit relying on my own wisdom and power and start relying on Yours instead.*

Do It 👣

Quit complaining about your problems; instead say, "Any problem that helps me lean on God more is an asset."

Day 19

No pain is wasted in God's economy.

Today's Verse

2 Corinthians 4:17–18 *"For our light and momentary troubles are achieving for us an eternal glory that far outweighs them all. So we fix our eyes not on what is seen, but on what is unseen. For what is seen is temporary, but what is unseen is eternal."*

Read About It 📖

Her troubles aren't light, Lord. She's wasting away! Cancer is ravaging her body. But inwardly she's growing. How odd it was to hear my dying friend say she had never felt more peaceful.

She really is looking at her troubles as light and momentary. She is recognizing how soon her faith will be rewarded in heaven. And she is fixing her eyes on Your glory, not on the radiation treatments, pain, or suffering that are to come. She knows that, unless You do a mighty miracle, soon she will get to see You face to face and spend forever in Your glorious presence. What a wonderful example of a Christian facing death enfolded in Your loving embrace.

But what about me, Lord? I'm not dying or even in pain. In light of what my friend is going through, I feel embarrassed to bring my little problems to You. What are You saying to me in today's verse?

The answer to my prayer was not audible, but I heard it clearly. God said,

"Your problems are important, too. Here is the secret of dealing with them: Don't focus on the external, but the eternal, my child."

Think About It

Paul is going through a rough time when he writes this passage. He says earlier in the chapter, "We are hard pressed on every side, but not crushed; perplexed, but not in despair; persecuted, but not abandoned; struck down, but not destroyed." But Paul knows how to keep his problems from getting him down. Here are Paul's principles:.

1. Paul considers his problems to be light. He is yoked to Jesus and allows Jesus to carry most of the load.

2. He considers his problems to be momentary. He has a heavenly perspective.

3. He considers his problems to be purposeful. He remembers that God has a purpose for all of his pain.

4. He fixes his eyes on eternal things, not external things. He focuses on the Lord and praises Him for His presence, His power, His plan, and His purpose.

Write About It ✏

As you answer these questions, consider each problem on the problem list you wrote yesterday.

Yes___ No___ 1. Rather than considering your problems to be light, do you make catastrophes of them—building them up rather than trusting Jesus to tear them down?

Yes___ No___ 2. Rather than considering your problems to be momentary, do you get so focused on them that time seems to stand still, like it does when you are waiting for a pot of water to boil?

Yes___ No___ 3. Rather than considering your problems to be purposeful, do you complain about your problems and refuse to learn from them?

Yes___ No___ 4. Rather than focusing on the eternal, do you let your thoughts remain on the superficial and external things of life almost all of the time?

Each of your *yes* answers will show you why your problems might be getting you down and your worries might be overwhelming you. Look back at Paul's principles (How to Keep Your Problems from Getting You Down) to learn how to change your *yes* answers to *no*.

There are other reasons why some people may worry more than others. Here are a few of them. Place a check next to any that pertain to you:

Why Some People Worry More Than Others

❑ 1. **Temperament**. People are born with different temperaments that help determine how they will react to life.
During the first few days of a baby's life, we can often
identify his or her temperament. Some babies are cheer-
ful and some are upset most of the time, even if they are
not in pain and all of their needs are being met. People
with melancholy temperaments have a tendency to focus
on their problems more than others.

❑ 2. **Childhood Stress**. People who experienced much stress
as children, such as those with abusive parents, will often
struggle more with worrying.

❑ 3. **Trauma**. People who have had a traumatic experience,
such as being in a war, being injured in an accident, or
being a victim of a crime, will often struggle more with
worry.

❑ 4. **Trials**. People who have experienced one trial after
another will often struggle more with worry. It is not sur-
prising that those with more to worry about will worry
more, but it doesn't have to be that way.

❑ 5. **Chemical Imbalance**. People with a history of chronic
depression, bipolar disorders, and other similar problems
often worry more. When their brain chemistry is correct-
ed, these people may find that they are able to stop worrying as much.

❑ 6. **PMS, Menopause**. During certain times of the month
and at certain times in their lives, women will be more
susceptible to worrying. Women in their mid to late 40's
and 50's need to be aware than menopausal depression
can occur even without all the other expected
menopausal changes. I have counseled any number of

women who suddenly began to feel overwhelmed with worries. Even women on Estrogen replacement therapy can experience this if their dosage is not high enough for them. If you are a woman in your 40's or 50's who normally does not worry a lot and you suddenly find that you can't stop worrying, consider discussing it with your gynecologist.

❏ 7. **Addictions**. Something is considered to be an addiction when you can't stop doing it even though it is harming you. All addictions, such as to drugs, alcohol, overeating, TV, the internet, busyness, or worrying, help the person to numb their thoughts so they don't have to think about their problems. Their worries grow, however, as the addiction takes over their lives. (It is odd that someone can become addicted to worrying, but I have seen this often. When people are addicted to worrying, they usually focus all their worries on things other than the real issue that is bothering them. For example, a 90-year-old may spend all his time worrying about saving enough money for his old age so that he doesn't have to face his fear of death.)

❏ 8. **Certain Behaviors**. (Check any of these that apply to you.)
There are many behaviors that contribute to worry.
❏ Disobeying the Lord
❏ Not having a daily quiet time
❏ Not confessing your sins
❏ Not having a close personal relationship with God
❏ Not accepting God's forgiveness
❏ Not forgiving others
❏ Beating yourself up for not being perfect
❏ Trying to hide things you are ashamed of
❏ Not casting your cares on the Lord

Other things we do also can make us worry more. Some examples are:

- ❑ Complaining
- ❑ Self-pity
- ❑ Procrastination
- ❑ Being around negative people
- ❑ Being around angry people
- ❑ Being too busy
- ❑ Being a perfectionist
- ❑ Being materialistic
- ❑ Not getting enough rest

Did any of the first six reasons why some people worry more than others apply to you? If they did, you need to watch that you don't use that reason as an excuse. For example, having a melancholy temperament is no excuse for worrying. It just means that you will have to work a little harder to stop.

Feel-Better Brain Chemicals

Doctors have discovered that certain brain chemicals, like serotonin, give us a feeling of well-being and help us not to worry as much. For one reason or another, some people have diminished levels of these feel-better brain chemicals. Here are some things that have been proven to boost these brain chemicals: (Check any you need to do more often)

- ❑ Pray and praise the Lord
- ❑ Laugh, play, have fun
- ❑ Do something relaxing, such as taking a long bath or getting a massage
- ❑ Arrange flowers, paint, or play the piano
- ❑ Listen to music you like
- ❑ Exercise, participate in sports

Pray About It

Tell God about the things you checked on the list titled Why
Some People Worry More Than Others. Ask Him to help you
to overcome the reason for worrying and not to use it as an
excuse.

_____

_____

_____

_____

_____

_____

_____

_____

Reflect on today's verse as you journey from worry to worship. 2 Corinthians 4:17–18 *"For our light and momentary
troubles are achieving for us an eternal glory that far outweighs them all. So we fix our eyes not on what is seen, but
on what is unseen. For what is seen is temporary, but what is
unseen is eternal."*

*Lord, thank You that my problems are light and momentary.
Some day they will end and I will look back on them and see
that You had a purpose and a plan for each of them. Help me
to fix my eyes on You and Your kingdom instead of my worries. Thank You that I am learning why I worry so much and
I am learning how to cooperate with You as You help me to
journey from worry to worship.*

Do It

Remember: Don't focus on the external, but the eternal!

Day 20

No pain is wasted in God's economy.

Today's Verse

Hebrews 12:10 *"Our fathers disciplined us for a little while as they thought best; but God disciplines us for our good, that we may share in his holiness."*

Read About It

I can't stand to be around undisciplined children. They always want and never give. They think only of themselves and focus so much on what they don't have, that they don't enjoy the things they have. They pout and whine. I feel sorry for them, though, because they are never satisfied and experience many negative consequences in life because they lack discipline.

It is easy for me to point fingers at them, but for many years, though I was grown, I was spiritually immature. Just like a spoiled child, I wanted what I wanted when I wanted it. I pouted and complained if I didn't get it. I was miserable because I was fighting God's discipline. I fell for the old lie that if God loved me, He would give me everything I wanted, and if He allowed unpleasant things to come into my life, it was because He didn't love me.

I am thankful that I finally began to understand today's verse and know that God disciplines me for my good, so that I may become more like Jesus and share in His holiness.

Think About It

This week we have focused on the thought that no pain is wasted in God's economy. Let me clarify one important point: No pain is wasted in God's economy—if God has His way—but that does not mean that no pain is ever wasted.

If we refuse to learn the lessons God is trying to teach us, He will give us opportunities to learn these lessons again and again. We will waste countless hours, days, and even years making the same mistakes and experiencing the same pain. If we don't discipline ourselves, God may have to do it for us.

But God is a wonderful Heavenly Father. He patiently and lovingly teaches us what we need to learn. He doesn't slap us with painful circumstances to get even with us. He allows challenges to come into our lives to help us to grow, to lean on Him, and to give our lives more meaning.

Look at the blessings that God tells us about in the verse following Today's Verse, Hebrews 12:11: "No discipline seems pleasant at the time, but painful. Later on, however, it produces a harvest of righteousness and peace for those who have been trained by it."

Do you want a harvest of righteousness and peace? Then let me give you some practical tips that will help you to be more disciplined.

Write About It

Start working toward your harvest by answering the following questions:

- What problems are you experiencing today? Make a list on another piece of paper. Include large and small problems.

- Put a star next to the problems you contributed to—for example, health problems that may be a result of an unhealthy lifestyle, an argument that occurred because you spoke without thinking, or financial problems that happened because you bought things you couldn't afford.

- Write by each starred problem how you contributed to it.

- Choose the two most significant problems that you contributed to and write small, achievable goals that will help you to deal with these problems constructively.

There are three things you need to consider when you make your goals:

1. **Make a goal that is achievable.** For example, don't say, "I will never scream at my children again." Instead, make an achievable goal, such as, "When I am angry at the children, I will take a time out so I can pray for a minute or two before I try to talk to them."

2. **Make a goal that is measurable.** For example, don't say, "I will spend less money." Instead, make a measurable goal, such as, "I will not buy things on credit."

3. **Make a goal that doesn't depend on another person.** For example, don't say, "My husband will lose weight." Instead, make a goal that governs only your actions, such as, "I will cook according to the food plan my husband's doctor gave him, and I will not buy cookies, candy, and chips."

- **Make a Victory List.** Keep a daily list of your goals. Every morning ask yourself if you achieved your goals the day before. If you did, put a big, bold check mark next to it! Congratulate yourself! (If you would like a Victory List form, visit www.worrytoworship.com)

Pray About It

Ask God to give you the willingness to become more disciplined. Be specific about areas that need attention. In addition, ask Him to help you to achieve the goals you have made.

_____

_____

_____

_____

_____

_____

_____

Reflect on today's verse as you journey from worry to worship. Hebrews 12:10 *"Our fathers disciplined us for a little while as they thought best; but God disciplines us for our good, that we may share in his holiness."*

Lord, You are a wonderful Heavenly Father. You love me just as I am, but You love me too much to leave me the way I am. Sometimes You allow problems to come into my life for other reasons, but often You send them to discipline me. Your discipline helps me to grow in faith, lets me know when I'm off track, and gives me the willingness to change. Help me to submit to Your discipline so I can experience a harvest of righteousness and peace as I journey from worry to worship.

Do It

Discipline yourself so God won't have to do it for you!

Chapter 5

God's Prize

Day 21
God will reward us.

Today's Verse

Isaiah 40:10 "*See, his reward is with him, and his recompense accompanies him.*"

Read About It

God will reward us when we go to heaven or when He comes to take us there. It will be joyous! No more sadness . . . no weakness . . . no pain . . . no unanswered questions. A glorious new life with Jesus. Think of it! Going to sleep tired and waking up transformed in the arms of your Savior!

In the Bible, God gives us several glimpses of how wonderful heaven will be.

In 2 Corinthians 5:1 (NLT) we are told about our new bodies. "*For we know that when this earthly tent we live in is taken down—when we die and leave these bodies—we will have a home in heaven, an eternal body made for us by God himself and not by human hands.*"

In the familiar 1 Corinthians 13:12 we are given two other exciting promises about heaven. "*Now we see but a poor reflection as in a mirror; then we shall see face to face.*

Now I know in part; then I shall know fully, even as I am fully known." (I can't wait to see Jesus face to face and to know "fully!" How wonderful it will be to be able to see Jesus and to ask Him anything I want to!)

In John 14:1–3, Jesus tells us about the beautiful home awaiting us and assures us that He will be with us. *"Let not your heart be troubled; you believe in God, believe also in Me. In My Father's house are many mansions; if it were not so, I would have told you. I go to prepare a place for you. And if I go and prepare a place for you, I will come again and receive you to Myself; that where I am, there you may be also. And where I go you know, and the way you know"* (NKJV).

In the last sentence, Jesus states two assumptions: that we know where He is going and how to get there. Thankfully, Thomas barges in and says something like, "Oh no we don't," so Jesus tells him more. Thanks to Thomas' question, Jesus makes one of the most important statements in the Bible.

In John 14:6, Jesus tells us how to get to heaven. He says: *"I am the way, the truth, and the life. No one comes to the Father except through Me"* (NKJV). He is telling us that He holds all the invitations to heaven in His hands, and He guards the gates so that only those of us who know Him may enter. (I can imagine the warm smile on His face as He welcomes us to our new home. What a wonderful reward we have waiting for us!)

Think About It

Do you want to know more about God's rewards? Here are three important facts, along with Scripture references that illumine each fact. Look up a few of them as you think about each fact.

1. Heaven is a gift that God gives to everyone who believes in His Son; it is not a reward for the good works that we do. (Ephesians 2:8-9, Romans 6:23, Romans 10:9)

2. We can build up our rewards in heaven while we are still on earth. (Matthew 6:19-20, Colossians 3:23-24, Matthew 5:11-12)

3. We will be rewarded for the good things we do. (Look how many times the Bible repeats the message found in today's verse! Isaiah 62:11, Jeremiah 17:10, Psalm 62:12, Ephesians 6:7-8, Matthew 16:27, Revelation 22:12)

God will reward us in heaven. We don't know what these rewards will be, but knowing God, we can be sure that they will be awesome! Let's journey from worry to worship by praising Him, in advance, for the prize that awaits us in heaven.

Write About It

Look at #2 above. Answer the following questions as they relate to the three passages found in that section.

Yes___ No___ 1. Are you focusing mainly on storing up for yourself treasures on earth?

Yes___ No___ 2. Do you worry a lot about "moth and rust" destroying your rewards?

Yes___ No___ 3. When you work, do you think about doing it with all your heart as if for the Lord?

4. If you worked as for the Lord, how would it help you?

_____

_____

Yes___ No___ 5. Has anyone ever insulted or persecuted you because of your stand for Christ?

Yes___ No___ 6. Rather than worrying about it, did you think about the reward that you would get in heaven because of it?

Yes___ No___ 7. Have you ever responded lovingly, out of
obedience to Christ, to someone who was
treating you unfairly?

When?_____

Pray About It 🙏

Reflect on today's verse as you journey from worry to worship. Isaiah 40:10 *"See, his reward is with him, and his recompense accompanies him."*

Tell God about any answers on the questionnaire that concern you. Ask Him to help you to journey from worry to worship in these areas.

_____

_____

_____

_____

Lord, thank You for overcoming death and my fear of it. Thank You that, because of what Jesus did for me on the cross, I don't have to worry about being good enough to go to heaven. And thank You for the exciting glimpses of heaven that You give me in the Bible. Help me to build up my rewards in heaven—to refuse to worry about storing up earthly treasures, to respond in love to those who are not being loving to me, and to work as if doing it for You.

Do It 👣

Work as if you are working for the Lord. It will lift your focus off of the ordinary and onto the holy.

Day 22
God will reward us.

Today's Verse

Psalm 84:11 *"No good thing does he withhold from those whose walk is blameless."*

Read About It

Today we are going to talk about the good things God gives us. Read this beautiful poem and be inspired to redefine the word "good." This anonymous poem is believed to have been found on the body of a Civil War soldier:

I asked God for strength, that I might achieve;
I was made weak, that I might learn humbly to obey.
I asked for health, that I might do greater things;
I was given infirmity, that I might do better things.
I asked for riches, that I might be happy;
I was given poverty, that I might be wise.
I asked for power, that I might have the praise of men;
I was given weakness, that I might feel the need of God.
I asked for all things, that I might enjoy life;
I was given life, that I might enjoy all things.
I got nothing that I asked for—but everything I had hoped for.
Almost despite myself, my unspoken prayers were answered.
I am, among all men, most richly blessed.

Think About It

God's idea of "good" and ours often are not the same. If we want to go from worry to worship, we need to redefine this word according to the definition used in the Kingdom of God, not in the world. Let's let Jesus help us to understand how to do this. Read His words recorded in Luke 6:20–26:

Blessed are you who are poor, for yours is the kingdom of God.
Blessed are you who hunger now, for you will be satisfied.
Blessed are you who weep now, for you will laugh.
Blessed are you when men hate you, when they exclude you
*   and insult you and reject your name as evil,*
*   because of the Son of Man.*
Rejoice in that day and leap for joy,
*   because great is your reward in heaven.*
For that is how their fathers treated the prophets.
But woe to you who are rich,
*   for you have already received your comfort.*
Woe to you who are well fed now, for you will go hungry.
Woe to you who laugh now, for you will mourn and weep.
Woe to you when all men speak well of you,
*   for that is how their fathers treated the false prophets.*

Being rich and being poor. The world says it's good to be rich, but Jesus says that if you are poor you can watch God supply what you need. He says that riches can cause you to turn to the world for your comfort (Luke 6:24), that it is hard for the rich to enter God's kingdom (Matthew 19:23–24) and that riches can be like thorns that choke out the seed of the Spirit growing in you (Matthew 13:22).

Paul says something about riches that is a paradox. He says that though he has nothing, he really possesses everything (2 Corinthians 6:10). Do you know what he means?

Being full and being hungry. Jesus tells you that if you are always full, you may never be satisfied. While searching for satisfaction, many people turn to the false satisfaction that food or other things provide instead of turning to the Lord. They spend their days hungry, but the more they eat, the hungrier they get. God wants you to hunger for righteousness (Matthew 5:6). When you do, you find true satisfaction that nourishes your soul (Psalm 63:5).

Being happy and weeping. The world tells you to seek happiness. Jesus says that if you do, you will end up weeping. He says for you not to seek happiness, but to seek Him (Matthew 6:33) and to cast your cares on Him (1 Peter 5:7). When you do, He will fill you with joy and other delightful spiritual fruit (John 15:5).

Being approved of or being hated. The world says to seek approval. God says not to (Galatians 1:10). He tells you to live at peace with everyone if you can (Romans 12:18), but to rejoice if people disapprove of you because you remind them of Jesus. Then He can reward you in heaven (Luke 6:23).

Being strong and being weak. The world says you should be strong. I have heard that the Bible verse that is quoted most often is: "God helps those who help themselves." This is not even in the Bible—it's an old saying from *Poor Richard's Almanac*, by Ben Franklin! As a matter of fact, the Bible says the exact opposite. Paul says that he rejoices in his weakness because it helps him to rely on God's strength (2 Corinthians 12:9).

Write About It

Certainly none of us would seek to be poor, hungry, weeping, hated, or weak, but if these things are part of our lives, God can work them together for good. Look at Romans 8:28 (NLT):

"And we know that God causes everything to work together for the good of those who love God and are called according to his purpose for them."

Yes___ No___ 1. Do you love God?

Yes___ No___ 2. Are you a Christian?

Yes___ No___ 3. Do you believe the Bible is true?

Yes___ No___ 4. Do you believe Romans 8:28 is true?

Yes___ No___ 5. Are you called according to God's purpose for your life?

Our hearts break when we think about people who are experiencing horrible trials. We don't understand how God could let these things happen and can't imagine how they can work together for good. But we must not allow ourselves to get stuck in this type of thinking. When these doubts come, we must not play god by telling ourselves that we would make wiser decisions than God. That kind of thinking is spiritual quicksand. Many people have gotten stuck there and have never gotten out. Our responsibility is to pray for hurting people and, if possible, do something to help them. We must remember the focus of today's lesson: the Kingdom of God often seems upside down to us. So let's praise God for His wisdom, even if we can't understand it, and ask Him to help us trust Him. I have a long list of questions to ask God when I get to heaven. I'll bet you do too!

If you have gotten stuck in spiritual quicksand or have No answers on your questionnaire above, talk to your pastor or a respected Christian friend about where you are. Begin praying that God will help you get unstuck so you can continue your journey from worry to worship.

Review the ten "good" things we discussed—five good things from the world's point of view and five good things from God's point of view. Answer the following questions, keeping in mind Romans 8:28.

Yes___ No___ 1. Are your thoughts constantly focused on money—striving to get more of it or worrying about not having enough?

Yes___ No___ 2. Are you usually miserable, searching for something (other than knowing God) that will make you feel satisfied?

Yes___ No___ 3. Do you spend too much time striving for happiness or worrying about not having it?

Yes___ No___ 4. Do you get completely overwhelmed when everyone doesn't approve of everything you say or do?

Yes___ No___ 5. Are you so ashamed of your weaknesses that you have given up on yourself?

Which of the five possible Yes answers above do you worry about most? _____

Write how God might be using this problem in your life.

_____

_____

_____

_____

_____

_____

_____

Pray About It 🙏

Reflect on today's verse as you journey from worry to worship. Psalm 84:11 *"No good thing does he withhold from those whose walk is blameless."*

Today's verse is the corollary to Romans 8:28. Let's see how they fit together.

Romans 8:28

Promise: Everything will work together for good in your life.

Condition: If you love God and want His will.

Result: You know that whatever happens to you, even if it seems bad, God can work it together for good.

Psalm 84:11

Promise: God won't withhold from you anything that is good.

Condition: If your walk is blameless. (That means if you are a Christian who tries to do God's will and confesses to Him when you sin.)

Result: You know that if you have prayed for something, but still don't have it, it probably isn't a good thing for you right now, or God wouldn't be withholding it.

Thank God for promising to work everything together for good in your life and promising to not withhold good things from you. Ask Him to help you to love Him, want His will, and walk blamelessly.

_____

_____

_____

_____

Thank You, Lord, for giving me the desire and ability to do Your will. And thank You that, because of what Jesus did for me on the cross, it is possible for me to walk blamelessly. Even though sometimes I don't understand why You allow things to happen as You do, I have faith that You know what You are doing. I praise You, Lord, for rewarding me both now and in heaven with good things.

Do It

Worry is never a good thing. The antidote to worry is worship, so get busy and praise God for the good things He is giving you!

Day 23
God will reward us.

Today's Verse

Hebrews 11:6 *"Without faith it is impossible to please God, because anyone who comes to him must believe that he exists and that he rewards those who earnestly seek him."*

Read About It

How would you feel if your little girl came to you with big tears falling down her face—worried about whether you would provide things she desperately needed? Even worse, how would you feel if she went next door for those things because she didn't want to bother you or she didn't think you would give them to her? It would break your heart.

That's what many of us do to God.

God tells us over and over again in the Bible that He will supply all our needs, yet we worry and fret about whether He really will. He says that He will reward us for our love and obedience, but because He is not rewarding us in the time or way of our choosing, we assume that He doesn't mean what He says. Or maybe we believe that His promises are for others, but not for us.

Today let's learn how to take God at His word. And as we grow in faith, I know we will be able to close our eyes and see a giant smile covering His face.

Think About It

Let's begin to stretch our faith by looking at today's verse again and asking ourselves some questions. Hebrews 11:6 *"Without faith it is impossible to please God, because anyone who comes to him must believe that he exists and that he rewards those who earnestly seek him."*

What is faith? Hebrews 11:1 tells us exactly what it is: *"Now faith is being sure of what we hope for and certain of what we do not see."*

Are there types of faith? Today's verse reminds me of four types of faith.

1. Those who come to God. When these people have a problem, they come searching for God, but when everything is okay, they don't think about Him.

2. Those who believe that God exists. When these people come to God, they find Him. They truly believe that He exists, but they don't use their faith in Him or develop a personal relationship with Christ. They might go to church every Sunday and occasionally read their Bibles, but their faith does not grow.

3. Those who earnestly seek Him. When these people come to God, they find Him. They believe that He exists, and they spend time seeking Him and studying His Word. They go to church and they develop a relationship with Christ, but still feel that they are missing out somehow. When troubles come, they often forget to turn to God and may secretly wonder whether He would help them even if they did.

4. Those who believe that God rewards those who earnestly seek Him. These people earnestly seek God daily through Bible study and prayer. They have a growing relationship with Christ and want to do His will. They sometimes stumble, but they confess their sins and feel confident that God forgives them. When these people have a problem, they turn to God and know that He will help them with it. Many times things they pray for don't happen as they wish, but they are thankful anyway. They know that God is blessing them while they are on earth and they are looking forward to going to heaven and receiving even bigger rewards there.

Why is faith so important? There are many reasons why faith is important. Today's verse gives us the most significant one: *"Without faith it is impossible to please God."* Without faith, we will not go to heaven when we die and we will not please God while we live. But another reason that faith is so important is that without it, we will fall prey to everything the devil hurls at us. We will live in hell on earth, overwhelmed by our problems and falling for the devil's lies.

Ephesians 6:16 tells us to *"take up the shield of faith, with which you can extinguish all the flaming arrows of the evil one."* In this passage, God gives us a wonderful word picture about how to fight the devil. He tells us to take up our shield of faith. Some people say they have faith, but they don't use it. God tells us to use our faith like a shield to protect us from the lies of the devil.

Write About It

We were just talking about something very important: spiritual warfare. Just as there is a Holy Spirit, the Bible tells us that there is an evil spirit that is trying to destroy us. Any time we start to grow in our faith, the devil comes against us. He has various tactics, but they always include his major weapon: lies. Those of us who tend to worry need to be even more aware of this weapon—this flaming arrow.

In the Garden of Eden, the devil lied to Eve about what God really said, and he lies to you and me about what God is saying to us today. Let's look at some of the devil's lies and the truth from God's Word. Place a check next to the lies you have fallen for:

Some of the Devil's Lies	The Truth from God's Word
God doesn't really love you. You don't deserve to go to heaven.	**John 3:16**— "For God so loved the world that he gave his one and only Son, that whoever believes in him shall not perish but have eternal life."
There is no way for you to trust God. You have always been a worrier and you can't change now.	**2 Corinthians 5:17**— "If anyone is in Christ, he is a new creation; the old has gone, the new has come!"
God won't help you. Your problems are too insignificant (or too hard) for Him to handle. He is busy with more important people.	**Isaiah 41:13**— "For I am the Lord, your God, who takes hold of your right hand and says to you, Do not fear; I will help you."
You are too busy to study the Bible and pray every day.	**Ephesians 3:20** (NLT)— "Now glory be to God! By his mighty power at work within us, he is able to accomplish infinitely more than we would ever dare to ask or hope."
God doesn't hear your prayers or notice when you do good things.	**1 Corinthians 2:9** (NLT)— "No eye has seen, no ear has heard, and no mind has imagined what God has prepared for those who love him."

Write, on another sheet of paper, about the lies of the devil that you checked. List other lies the devil is telling you.

Below you will find the four types of faith we discussed. Where are you in your faith?
1. Those who come to God
2. Those who believe that God exists
3. Those who earnestly seek Him
4. Those who believe that God rewards those who earnestly seek Him

Pray About It

Write your prayer telling God about your type of faith. Ask Him to help your faith to grow.

As you review the section titled "The Devil's Lies and the Truth from God's Word," thank God for the verse that you needed to hear most today.

Reflect on today's verse as you journey from worry to worship. Hebrews 11:6 *"Without faith it is impossible to please God, because anyone who comes to him must believe that he exists and that he rewards those who earnestly seek him."*

Lord, please help my faith to grow. Help me to trust You more and more, no matter my circumstances. Help me to think about how sad my lack of faith must make You so I will be motivated to confess my worries and replace them with worship. And help me to cooperate with You as You increase my faith—to spend time praising You, studying Your Word, asking for Your help, and clinging to Your truth rather than the lies the devil is telling me. Father, I want my faith to please You. Thank You for understanding the magnetic pull that sin has on me and for helping me to break loose from the things that are getting me down.

Do It

When a worry strikes, ask yourself if it is based on God's truth or one of the devil's lies.

Day 24
God will reward us.

Today's Verse

Psalm 37:3–4 *"Trust in the Lord and do good; dwell in the land and enjoy safe pasture. Delight yourself in the Lord and he will give you the desires of your heart."*

Read About It

God never tells us to do something without supplying exactly what we need to do it. In today's verse God tells us how to trust Him—to make the journey from worry to worship. Here are four Trust Builders that come from today's verse.

Trust Builders

1. Do good. If we want to trust God—to relax in Him, to quit worrying and feeling so stressed—we must obey Him. Fortunately, this doesn't mean that we have to fix the times when we didn't obey Him in the past or that we will always do it perfectly in the future. It means that we must sincerely seek to do God's will, and when we don't do it, we must confess our sins to Him and begin again seeking to do His will.

2. Dwell in the land. Spending eternity in the Kingdom of God does not begin when we die; it begins the second we confess Christ as our Savior. We can dwell in the land—His promised land—right now as we walk in His Spirit, relying on Him to lead us and empower us to do His will.

3. Enjoy safe pasture. We enjoy the safe pasture we are living in by constantly keeping Romans 8:28 in mind. When we love God and want His will, we can be assured that He will work everything out in our lives for good.

4. Delight yourself in the Lord. We do this as we praise God for His Presence, His Power, His Plan, His Purpose, and His Prize. We also delight ourselves in the Lord in other ways, such as by going to church, studying His Word, praying, and working as unto the Lord. Notice the wonderful promise that comes when we delight ourselves in the Lord: He will give us the desires of our heart.

A Secret I Learned

As you use the four Trust Builders, you will find that your desires change. I found that out while I was battling my cravings for fattening foods. The doctor said that I had to lose weight so my blood pressure would go down.

By using these Trust Builders and other biblical principles, I found that I started craving healthier foods. For example, I began to long for fresh fruit cocktail and grilled shrimp. And I no longer wanted things that were not good for me. After eating my healthier foods for a while, I would be turned off by fatty foods or foods with too much sugar. It is an amazing fact, but it's true. God changed my desires to match His.

If you haven't discovered that God will change your desires, keep using these Trust Builders and you'll see!

Think About It

Here are some ways to develop the four Trust Builders:

1. Do good Think of a sin that you continue to commit—for instance, maybe you have a bad temper, a problem with resentment, or maybe you are having a physical relationship outside of marriage. Write God a letter about this. Ask Him to give you the willingness and ability to change. Keep a record of any progress that you are making in this area. Praise God that He loves you despite your sin, but that He loves you too much to leave you in it.

2. Dwell in the land. In the previous section, I mentioned that we can dwell in God's promised land when we walk in His Spirit. We have only two choices—two places we can walk: His Spirit or our flesh. Practice walking in His Spirit.

3. Enjoy safe pasture. You will enjoy safe pasture when you walk close to your Shepherd—remembering that He is providing what you need and protecting you from wasted pain or meaningless wandering. If you go outside of His will or rely on other people or things to make you safe, you will never feel secure.

4. **Delight yourself in the Lord.** Note serendipities that remind you of God. A serendipity is a pleasant surprise. Sing praise songs at the top of your lungs as you drive your car. Tell someone about the wonderful things God is doing in your life today, even if your circumstances are difficult. Do a good deed without letting anyone know you did it.

Write About It

We said that there are only two places we can walk: in God's Spirit or in the flesh. We also talked about Trust Builders—things that encourage us to walk in God's Spirit. Let's look at some Flesh Builders—thoughts that encourage us to walk in the flesh and find our security there. Place a check next to Flesh Builders that you recognize in your life.

Flesh Builders
   ❑ I must build up my bank account to feel secure.
   ❑ I must have compliments and appreciation to feel secure.

❑ I must have control of my job and family to feel secure.
❑ I must not have changes to feel secure.
❑ I must turn to an addiction to feel secure.
❑ I must do things perfectly to feel secure.
❑ I must have no problems to feel secure.
❑ I must stay busy to feel secure.
❑ I must ignore my mistakes to feel secure.
❑ I must blame others to feel secure.

Write about the Flesh Builders you checked and why these thoughts keep you from experiencing real security

_____

_____

_____

_____

Pray About It 🙏

Ask God to help you to find your security in Him, not in things of the flesh.

_____

_____

_____

_____

Reflect on today's verse as you journey from worry to worship. Psalm 37:3–4 *"Trust in the Lord and do good; dwell in the land and enjoy safe pasture. Delight yourself in the Lord and he will give you the desires of your heart."*

I have taken God's words from today's verse and rewritten them as if God were speaking to you today . . . and He is!

*Dear (Insert your name)*_____,
*Trust Me and do what is right. Stay close to Me and enjoy the
fact that I am taking care of you. Delight yourself in Me—in
My presence with you, My power at work in you, My plan for
your life, My purpose for your pain, and My prize—the reward
I am giving you now and the ones I will give you in heaven.
Don't ever forget My awesome promise: if you delight yourself
in Me, I will give you the desires of your heart.*

> *Love,*
> *God*

Do It

Don't delight yourself in the world and expect God to give
you the desires of your heart.

Day 25
God will reward us.

Today's Verse

2 Timothy 4:7–8 *"I have fought the good fight,
I have finished the race, I have kept the faith.
Now there is in store for me the crown of righteousness, which the Lord, the righteous Judge,
will award to me on that day."*

Read About It

I always think of Aunt Mary when I read today's verse. How I want to finish well like she did! Aunt Mary wasn't really my aunt. She didn't have any nieces or nephews, so my mother encouraged me to call her Aunt Mary even though she was only my double second cousin. (I never did figure out the "double" part, but that's what Mom always said she was.)

Though by earthly standards, Aunt Mary had little—no husband or children, not much money—she was consistently joyful. She had a positive attitude even when others would have fallen into fretting and self-pity.

She faithfully played the organ for her church for 40 years, but was suddenly "let go" because they wanted something more modern than the heart-felt hymns Aunt Mary played. That didn't get her off track for a minute. Neither did the other trial that followed on the heels of her lost job.

When Aunt Mary's only brother was wasting away with cancer, she sat for months in the nursing home reading *The Living Bible* to him cover to cover. Every time I saw her, she always mentioned the same two things: how wonderful it was to read God's Word in such a fresh, new way and how exciting it was that her brother would soon be meeting the Lord face to face.

Even when going through painful trials like these, her eyes sparkled as she talked about how good the Lord had been to her. She praised Him at every opportunity . . . sometimes to people who didn't feel like praising Him back, but that didn't slow my Aunt Mary down.

At 89, she had prepared a dinner party for 20 guests on Christmas day, but no one showed up. A blizzard isolated her in that big old white house where she was born and spent all of her days. Christmas day came and went and she remained all alone. When the phone lines were repaired and I got in touch with her the day after Christmas, she said, "Oh, Jesus and I had such a wonderful celebration of His birthday. Just Him and me. It was really special!"

Oh yes, I do want to imitate my Aunt Mary. She fought a good fight. She kept the faith. She finished the race. And at age 90, as if God personally sent His chariot for her, she died instantly when a big truck smashed her rickety old Ford. We always told her she drove too slowly on those big highways, but she kept chugging along as she always had, and God took her home.

She is now experiencing everything that He promised her. I'll bet she's having a ball with Him in heaven. I can't wait to see the sparkle in her eyes as she tells me all about it.

Think About It

Today's verse talks about finishing well. When Paul wrote these words, he was in chains in a dingy dungeon—awaiting his execution. He was looking back on his life, as most people do when they are facing death.

I worked in a hospital intensive care unit for many years and talked to a lot of people who, like Paul, were looking back on their lives as they faced death. Many of them expressed regrets. They talked sadly about things that they didn't do that they wished they had and about the God they never really knew. A lot of them talked about running the Rat Race and wistfully confessed that it never got them anywhere.

I don't want to look back on my life with regret. I'll bet you don't either. We want to be able to say, like Paul, that we have fought a good fight, finished the race, and kept the faith. Let's do something about it now so that when our time comes, we won't regret running the Rat Race instead of the Right Race.

"How will talking about this help me not to worry?" Marge asked one afternoon in the counseling office of my church where she had come to me for help. Marge, a heavy-set woman in her 50's, had just told me that she felt overwhelmed most of the time—constantly busy, but getting nowhere.

"Marge," I answered thoughtfully, "you just described running the Rat Race—constantly busy, but getting nowhere. As long as you run the Rat Race and not the Right Race, you will not find God's peace. Let's get busy and see where you got off track and what you can do to get back on."

Run the Right Race, Not the Rat Race
Contrast the Rat Race and the Right Race. Place a check next to the things in either column that you do.

The Rat Race	The Right Race
1. Gather as many possessions as you can so you'll feel good about yourself.	1. Don't base your worth on your possessions or bank account. Base it on the fact that you are loved by God.
2. Make sure that you impress other people by what you have or do.	2. Rejoice in the fact that you please God because you are His. Aim to please Him even more with your thoughts, words, and deeds.
3. Depend on your wisdom, strength, and other personal attributes to assure your success.	3. Depend on God to help you to do His will and reward you for cooperating with Him.
4. Stay busy so you will get a lot done.	4. Spend time every day praying and studying God's Word to help you find the direction and ability to do the things God has called you to do.
5. When you fail, make excuses, blame others, or fall into shame.	5. When you fail, ask God to show you your mistake, confess your sin, and rejoice that God will work your mistake out for good because you love Him and want His will.

Look at two other passages in which Paul tells us how to run the Right Race.

1 Corinthians 9:26-27

How to Run the Right Race	Applications
1 Corinthians 9:26 (NLT)— "So I run straight to the goal with purpose in every step."	Have goals and don't wander aimlessly away from them like a runner who forgets where the finish line is.
1 Corinthians 9:26 (NLT)— "I am not like a boxer who misses his punches."	Don't play at being a Christian like a boxer who is just shadowboxing.
1 Corinthians 9:27 (NLT)— "I discipline my body like an athlete, training it to do what it should."	Be disciplined through Bible study and prayer so you can stay in shape spiritually.

Hebrews 12:1-2

How to Run the Right Race	Applications
Hebrews 12:1— "Therefore, since we are surrounded by such a great cloud of witnesses . . ."	Be encouraged by Christians who have gone before you and who surround you now.
Hebrews 12:1— "Let us throw off everything that hinders and the sin that so easily entangles . . ."	Confess your sins and let go of everything that prevents you from running the Right Race.
Hebrews 12:1— "And let us run with perseverance the race marked out for us."	Keep running the race that God marked out for you, even when it hurts.
Hebrews 12:2— "Let us fix our eyes on Jesus, the author and perfecter of our faith . . ."	Keep your focus on Jesus. Remember He gave you your faith and will help it to grow if you cooperate with Him.
Hebrews 12:2— "Who for the joy set before him endured the cross, scorning its shame, and sat down at the right hand of the throne of God."	As you pick up your cross daily and follow Him, don't forget the reward that awaits you in heaven.

Write About It

Answer the following questions as you consider each of the applications we just made on the Right Race verses.

1. Have goals and don't wander aimlessly away from them, like a runner who forgets where the finish line is. Do you have any goals that will help you grow spiritually? What are they?

2. Don't play at being a Christian like a boxer who is just shadowboxing. Has your religion really just been religiosity (religiosity is following rules, not seeking a real relationship with Jesus Christ)?

3. Be disciplined through Bible study and prayer so you can stay in shape spiritually. In the last 25 days, while studying *From Worry to Worship*, have you become more disciplined? In what ways?

4. Be encouraged by Christians who have gone before you and who surround you now. Have you ever had a mentor to help you grow in your faith? If you wanted to have a mentor now, who would you ask?

5. Confess your sins and let go of everything that prevents you from running the Right Race. Do you have a specific time every day to confess your sins? Do you take inventory from time to time to check the direction of your life?

6. Keep running the race that God marked out for you, even when it hurts. If God calls you to do something that is hard, do you give up and quit? What challenging thing is God calling you to do now?

7. Keep your focus on Jesus. Remember He will help you to grow if you cooperate with Him. Do you cooperate with God most of the time, or do you play tug of war with Him? What are you holding on to that He wants you to put down?

Pray About It

Review the questionnaire for today. Confess ways you have been running the Rat Race. Ask God to help you to run the Right Race. List specific things you will do to run the Right Race.

_____

_____

_____

_____

Reflect on today's verse as you journey from worry to worship. 2 Timothy 4:7–8 *"I have fought the good fight, I have finished the race, I have kept the faith. Now there is in store for me the crown of righteousness, which the Lord, the righteous Judge, will award to me on that day."*

Lord, let the words in today's verse be the words I say when I am facing my own death. Help me to finish the race—the Right Race—and quit running the Rat Race so I won't have to live in worries and regrets. Show me the things that are hindering my race, Lord. Help me to put them down so I can run well and receive the rewards that You have waiting for me in heaven.

Do It

Run the Right Race, not the Rat Race.

Chapter 6

God's Promises

Day 26

His Word is trustworthy;
it gives us something tangible to hold on to
when we are stepping out in faith.

Today's Verse

Isaiah 40:8 *"The grass withers and the flowers fall, but the word of our God stands forever."*

Read About It

This is a frightening time in which we live. Wars and rumors of wars. Terrorists who could strike at any moment. Financial meltdowns. Natural disasters. Epidemics. News commentators predicting catastrophes 24 hours a day or gleefully reporting the latest one. Yes, these are frightening times. But we have something to hold on to so we won't be overwhelmed with worries.

We can cling to God's promises. When we learn how to trust God's Word, our worries begin to fade and we are able feel certain in these uncertain times.

God gives us hundreds of comforting word pictures that help us to trust in His protection. We will explore many of them this week. We will also learn exciting new ways to study God's Word so we can apply it to the particular worries we are facing.

Today's verse draws an encouraging word picture for us. It tells us that God's Word will stand forever. It won't be changed, altered, or superseded. And it won't be pushed down, shoved away, or toppled over. No matter what happens, God's Word will always stand, and if we cling to it, we will too.

Think About It

Let's look at two other passages that draw pictures that encourage us to rely on God's Word.

- **Hebrews 6:18–19** (NLT) "We who have fled to him for refuge can take new courage, for we can hold on to his promise with confidence. This confidence is like a strong and trustworthy anchor for our souls."

- **Psalm 119:165** "Great peace have they who love your law, and nothing can make them stumble."

I want to teach you an exciting new way to apply God's Word to the problems that you are facing today. We will practice with today's verse and the other passage that we just mentioned.

Structured Meditation
Many people are able to apply the Bible to their own lives in a deeper way by using structured meditations. The word *meditation* means "to ponder." In Joshua 1:8 God tells us that if we meditate on His Word day and night, we will be prosperous and successful. We could all use that!

> **To do a structured meditation, write the answers to these six questions:**
> 1. What is the promise (either implied or stated) in the verse?
> 2. What is the command (either implied or stated)?
> 3. What questions does this verse bring to my mind?
> 4. How do I claim the promise?
> 5. How do I commit to the command?
> 6. What do I want to say to God about this verse?

Have you noticed that most verses in the Bible come with a promise and command? Sometimes they are implied, but they are almost always there. It is important not to separate the promise from the command. In other words, don't claim the promise without committing to obey the command.

Write About It

Let's practice doing a structured meditation with today's verse.
Isaiah 40:8 *"The grass withers and the flowers fall, but the word of our God stands forever."*

1. What is the promise (either implied or stated) in the verse?
   - The promise is "the word of our God stands forever."

2. What is the command (either implied or stated)?
   There is no right or wrong answer here, but I believe that the implied command is to put your trust in God's Word.
   - What do you think it is? _____

3. What questions does this verse bring to my mind?
   Some questions that come to my mind are:
   - Am I putting my trust in things that will wither and fall?
   - If so, what are they?

4. How do I claim the promise that the Word of God stands forever?

   - Think about one of God's promises you had given up on, but after awhile it happened anyway. (The promise that I had given up on was that I would be stand up against the temptation to overeat—1 Corinthians 10:13.)

   - What was a promise you had given up on, but later watched it happen?

   _____

5. How do I commit to the command?

   - One of the ways I can commit to the command (to put my trust in God's Word) is by committing to spend a certain time every day studying it and writing meditations on it.

   - How do you commit to this command?

   _____

6. What do I want to say to God about this verse?

   Here is a Letter to God that might be similar to one you would write about this verse:

   Lord, thank You for Your Word, which will never fail. When I look at this chaotic world around me, I need to hold on to something that will always stand. I can't rely on anything else and feel secure. My bank account is withering and the stock market is falling, but I want to trust in Your Word and know that You will provide everything I need.

   ### Now you try one!

Here is another word picture that will encourage you to trust in God's Word. Psalm 119:165 *"Great peace have they who love your law, and nothing can make them stumble."*

1. What are the promises? (There are two of them.)

   - _____
   - _____

2. What is the implied command?

* _____

3. What questions does this verse bring to my mind? (Hint: God's law is referring to His Word.)

* _____
* _____

4. How do I claim the promises?

* _____
* _____

5. How do I commit to the command?

* _____
* _____

6. What do I want to say to God about this verse?

_____

_____

_____

(For my answers and another structured meditation example, visit www.worrytoworship.com.)

Pray About It

Think about both of the word pictures from the Bible that we studied today:

1. The Word will stand forever even when other things wither and fall—**Isaiah 40:8**.
2. The Word is what keeps me from stumbling—**Psalm 119:165**.

Write a thank you note to God for what His Word is doing for you today.

_____

_____

_____

_____

Reflect on today's verse as you journey from worry to worship. Isaiah 40:8 *"The grass withers and the flowers fall, but the word of our God stands forever."*

Thank You, Father, for Your Word. It always stands, it makes me secure, and it keeps me from stumbling. It gives me something tangible to hold on to as I step out in faith and face each new day. Help me to use it, treasure it, trust it, study it, cling to it, obey it, and share it with others.

Do It

Psalm 119:105 says that God's Word is a light for your path, so don't ignore it and then complain when you fall down.

_____

Day 27

His Word is trustworthy;
it gives us something tangible to hold on to
when we are stepping out in faith.

Today's Verse

Isaiah 40:31 *(KJV) "But they that wait upon the Lord shall renew their strength; they shall mount up with wings as eagles; they shall run, and not be weary; and they shall walk, and not faint."*

Read About It 📖

Waiting is hard. Time drags. Hope fades. Worries mount. Some of us have been waiting a long time for important things to happen . . . and nothing does.

Why would God make us wait and be so uncomfortable? Today's verse has a sister verse that answers that question.

Deuteronomy 32:11

[The Lord is] "like an eagle that stirs up its nest and hovers over its young, that spreads its wings to catch them and carries them on its pinions."

Eagles build large nests. They use the same ones year after year, and each year they add to their nests. Some of them grow to be 10 feet across and 20 feet deep. Lined with fur and feathers, they are very comfortable—at least for eagles. The parents hover over their baby eaglet, constantly feeding him and taking care of his needs. But after 12 weeks or so, everything changes. The mother and father eagle bring food, but not all the way into the nest. They hold it out where the eaglet can see it, but they don't give it to him. And the mother eagle begins to stir up the nest. She removes its soft lining so sharp sticks that form the nest's foundation prick the baby eagle.

That really makes the eaglet uncomfortable. He liked living in his soft, cozy nest, all safe and secure, tummy full. His discomfort drives him to the edge of the nest and he perches precariously there—usually high in a tree or a cliff. He squawks for food, but the parents make him wait . . . and wait.

Eventually, if he refuses to budge, his mother beats him out of the nest with her strong wings. How confusing this must be for the eaglet. As he tumbles toward the rocks below, he is filled with unanswered questions: Why would his mother make him leave his cozy nest? But as he plunges head over heels toward certain death, his mother swoops down under him and catches him on her back.

"Ahh," the eaglet says to himself, "Mama is taking me back to the nest . . . but wait, we passed the nest and we're going even higher . . . Oh no! She's going to drop me again!" And he goes tumbling toward earth. But this time he looks at his mother flying next to him and sees how she puts her wings out and glides. And he tries it, too, and learns something amazing. He can fly!

Think About It

This passage draws a heart-warming picture of the Lord, who makes us wait for the things we want and stirs up our comfy little nest. If we still refuse to leave, He shoves us out because He loves us too much to let us stay there. The Lord hovers over us, and even when He seems to be doing things to hurt us and cause us to fall, He is always there, ready to catch us on His wings and carry us to safety.

Today's verse also refers to eagle wings. It tells us that if we wait upon the Lord, we can do things we never imagined possible. We can "mount up with wings as eagles"—we can glide over things that would have worn us out before. We can "run and not be weary." And when our circumstances slow down and our routine drags monotonously, we can do something even harder, we can "walk and not faint"—patiently facing the demanding boss, the lingering health problem, or the income that won't stretch far enough.

While we are waiting on the Lord, we can use our time wisely instead of wasting it squawking on the side of the nest. We can quit holding on to our old ways and put our hope in the Lord, who will teach us to fly.

God is never late, but His people often have to wait to see His promises. Abraham waited for the birth his son almost 25 years after receiving God's promise, and Moses waited 40 years in exile. But if you are waiting upon the Lord, your time is well spent. If you are waiting on the world, it is often wasted.

Write About It ✎

• What are you waiting for? _____
_____

• Are you waiting upon the Lord or the world? _____

Place a check next to the answers that apply to you.

Those Who Wait upon the World Wait This Way	Those Who Wait upon the Lord Wait This Way
Put their hope in people or things.	Put their hope in the Lord.
Look at waiting as a waste of time.	Look at waiting as an important time to use, preparing for what is to come.
Wait passively, regretting what might have been.	Wait proactively, changing things that have been holding them down.
Wait impatiently.	Wait expectantly.
Complain about what they lack.	Rejoice that the Lord will provide what they need.
Feel imprisoned by their thoughts—chained to irritation and aggravation.	Capture their thoughts—turn their worry to worship.

Things That Keep You from Soaring

When you wait upon the Lord, your strength will be renewed. You will find qualities and abilities you never knew you had and you will soar. But there are several things that hold you down and, like squawking eaglets, keep you perched sadly on the side of your nest. Let's explore some of them. Place a check next to the main quality that you have in common with a squawking eaglet. If you are sure that you don't have any of these qualities, go to the next section.

1. Anger
2. Complaining
3. Self-pity

4. Laziness
5. Complacency
6. Fear of change

Qualities of a squawking eaglet	Practical tip that will help you to soar
Anger	Make a list of people with whom you are angry and write a prayer telling God what they did to make you angry. Then write a prayer asking God to help you to forgive them in the same way that He has forgiven you.
Complaining	Instead of dumping your negative feelings on others, write a letter to God about them. If you have a legitimate complaint, pray about it and then share it with the person involved by telling him or her the truth in love.
Self-pity	Write God a list of reasons for your self-pity and ask Him to help you to have an attitude of gratitude. Then ask God to show you one or two things on your list that you can change with His help and begin changing those things.
Laziness	Confess your laziness to God and write a list of ways that you have been lazy. Make a goal to work on one of these things for a certain amount of time every day. (For example, if your house is a mess, make a goal to clean it for an hour a day.)
Complacency	Confess your complacency to God and write a list of ways that it is harming you. Write a prayer asking God to help you to grow and to step out in faith. Read it every day for a month.
Fear of change	Write God about things you fear might happen if you change and ask Him for courage. Write the primary thing that you know God wants you to change and then write baby steps you can take toward changing it. Take one of those baby steps today!

Pray About It 🙏

Reflect on today's verse as you journey from worry to worship. Isaiah 40:31 (KJV) *"But they that wait upon the Lord shall renew their strength; they shall mount up with wings as eagles; they shall run, and not be weary; and they shall walk, and not faint."*

Write your prayer, telling God ways you have been waiting on the world. Ask Him to help you to wait on Him instead.

_____

_____

_____

_____

Lord, thank You for the wonderful promise of eagle wings. Help me not to waste them like a squawking eaglet who sits on the side of the nest rather than soaring freely like You created me to do. Give me the willingness to spend my time in work and worship while I wait on You. Help me to have the courage to change, to leap out in faith, and to try new things that You are leading me to do.

Do It 👣

Praise the Lord while you wait upon Him. He is never late.

Day 28
His Word is trustworthy;
it gives us something tangible to hold on to
when we are stepping out in faith.

Today's Verse

Psalm 63:7–8 *"Because you are my help, I sing in the shadow of your wings. My soul clings to you; your right hand upholds me."*

Read About It

Today's verses are my life verses. I chose them prayerfully and carefully almost 30 years ago. I decided that they expressed what I wanted the theme of my life to be—a lifestyle of intimacy with God—living in God's shadow, relying on His help, singing and clinging to Him, trusting Him to always uphold me.

Since choosing this passage, I have been purposefully seeking ways to make my life reflect these words. But because I had always been a worrier, this was especially hard for me. How I longed for a button I could push that would help me to trust God more! I didn't find something as quick and easy as a Trust Button, but I have found many things I could do to help me to trust God more. I have shared a lot of them with you, but there are two more I want to share with you today: "Resigning from the Judgment Committee" and "Acting As If." Let me tell you how I learned these two Trust Builders.

I told you that my doctor led me to the Lord 30 years ago, but I didn't tell you how he almost had to drag me to Christ. Every time Dr. Jones talked about Jesus, I would bring up the ton of worries I had been clinging to about religion. Things like: "How can bad things happen to good people?" "Will natives who never heard about Jesus go to heaven?" "Why are some Christians so hypocritical?" and "How can I be sure that God really exists anyway?"

I was so focused on my worries that I was unable to focus

on the real question: Where could I find the lasting peace and power that I so desperately needed?

Dr. Jones realized that as long as I held on to my worries about religion, I would never be able to cling to my Savior. So he told me to do two things: the first thing he said was . . .

• Resign from the Judgment Committee. Dr. Jones told me to let God be God and to quit trying to figure Him out or judge whether He was doing a good job.

The second thing he told me to do was . . .

• Act As If. Dr Jones told me to act as if I believed that Jesus was God's Son and that He died so that I could be forgiven for my sins and find power over them. He said for me to pray and read the Bible for a few minutes every day, acting as if I was sure that this would help me to know God better. And he also encouraged me to act as if I believed that God was with me all the time to help me. So I started Acting As If and I resigned from the Judgment Committee.

After a short time, I started noticing exciting changes. I worried less and felt peace and joy more. I somehow knew that what I was doing would help me to quit being a worrywart and start being a worshipper. It has been a long journey from worry to worship . . . and I am still on it. But what a wonderful journey it is!

Think About It

Let's study 2 Corinthians 10:5 to learn more about resigning from the Judgment Committee and Acting As If.

2 Corinthians 10:5

"We demolish arguments and every pretension that sets itself up against the knowledge of God, and we take captive every thought to make it obedient to Christ."

I believe that *"Demolishing arguments and every pretension that sets itself up against the knowledge of God"* means to quit arguing with God's Word and pretending that we know better than God.

That is exactly what I was doing when I questioned God's existence and His wisdom. But when I resigned from the Judgment Committee and began Acting As If I believed God's Word, even though I couldn't understand some of it, it was like God opened His floodgates and faith rushed forth.

The second half of 2 Corinthians 10:5, "We take captive every thought to make it obedient to Christ," has helped me more than any other verse to journey from worry to worship.

Because of this verse, I realized several things:

• I realized that I could capture my thoughts. Before, I believed that I was powerless over the thoughts and worries that zoomed around in my brain.

• I realized that what I was thinking wasn't necessarily what I really believed. Lots of my thoughts were left over from my old way of thinking, and other thoughts were lies the devil was telling me.

• This verse also helped me to know what to do with my negative thoughts to keep them from overpowering me. I began to treat them like prisoners of war in the battle in my mind.

Here is what I do when I am worried:

1. Write my thoughts down.

2. Examine them to see whether they agree with God's Word or if they are lies of the devil.

3. If they don't agree with the Bible, I turn them around and make them obedient to Christ by replacing the captured thought with a promise from the Bible.

4. I memorize the promise so that when the thought comes back, I can continue to turn it around and make it obedient to Christ.

Write About It

Focus on today's verse as you practice taking your worries captive and making them obedient to Christ. Psalm 63:7–8— "Because you are my help, I sing in the shadow of your wings. My soul clings to you; your right hand upholds me."

1. "Because you are my help." What are you worrying about today? Capture these worries and make them obedient to Christ by using these or other Bible verses. Put a check next to anything you are worrying about. Memorize the verse that corresponds with your greatest worry.

War, terrorism	**Psalm 62:1–2** "My soul finds rest in God alone; my salvation comes from him. He alone is my rock and my salvation; he is my fortress, I will never be shaken."
Old age	**Isaiah 46:4**— "Even to your old age and gray hairs I am he, I am he who will sustain you. I have made you and I will carry you; I will sustain you and I will rescue you."
Children not walking with Jesus	**Isaiah 44:3**— "For I will pour water on the thirsty land, and streams on the dry ground; I will pour out my Spirit on your offspring, and my blessing on your descendants."
Money	**Hebrews 13:5**— "Keep your lives free from the love of money and be content with what you have, because God has said, 'Never will I leave you; never will I forsake you.'"
Disapproval	**Hebrews 13:6**— "So we say with confidence, 'The Lord is my helper; I will not be afraid. What can man do to me?'"
Unfair treatment	**Genesis 50:20**— "You intended to harm me, but God intended it for good to accomplish what is now being done."

2. "I sing in the shadow of your wings." The second phrase of Today's Verse reminds me of the importance of singing God's praises instead of complaining.

Questionnaire	Practical Tips
Yes___ No___ Instead of singing in God's shadow, are you complaining?	1. Every morning pray that God will set a guard over your mouth (Psalm 141:3). 2. Make a goal to cut back on complaining. Use a Victory List daily to check how you are doing (see Day 20).
Yes___ No___ Do you worry that you are often a negative witness to others?	1. Remember that you are always in God's shadow. 2. Ask God to help you to reflect Him with your words, attitudes, and actions.

3. "My soul clings to you." Don't just think about God; cling to Him—hold fast to Him and don't let go by trying to fight your battles alone.

Questionnaire	Practical Tips
Yes___ No___ When you are worried, do you usually think about God?	Act as if you believe that God will help you with every problem. Here is how to Act As If: • Cling to God's promises. • Speak positively. • Trust God to help you change the things you can. • Give things you can't change to Him to take care of.
Yes___ No___ Have you memorized a verse to help you to deal with your worries?	Choose one to memorize today! Memorize a verse every day for three minutes.
Yes___ No___ Do you question God and distance yourself from Him when He doesn't answer your prayers as you asked?	Resign from the Judgment Committee. Quit judging God. Instead, praise Him that He knows best.

4. "Your right hand upholds me." God's right hand will keep you from falling into sin. Jesus is sitting at God's right hand.

Questionnaire	Practical Tips
Yes___ No___ When you are tempted to sin, do you usually pray for help?	1. Make a list of temptations you face. Write a prayer, in advance, for each one. 2. When you actually are in the midst of temptation, repeat what you told God earlier.
When you are in the midst of an argument or misunderstanding, do you usually pray silently for wisdom? Yes___ No___	1. Any time there is a disagreement, pray silently that God will keep you from falling into things like blaming, criticizing, and belittling. 2. If things are getting too difficult, excuse yourself to go to the bathroom. You don't have to say that you are going there to pray.

Pray About It

Reflect on today's verse as you journey from worry to worship. Psalm 63:7–8 *"Because you are my help, I sing in the shadow of your wings. My soul clings to you; your right hand upholds me."*

Refer to today's questionnaire and consider answers that concern you. Ask God to help you to grow in those areas. Tell Him about any of the practical tips that you would like to try.

_____

_____

_____

_____

Thank You, Father, for being my help. When I have doubts, help me to Act As If I believe by clinging to Your promises and singing Your praises to myself and others. And when I am disappointed over unanswered prayers, help me to resign from the

Judgment Committee and praise You because You know best. Help me to take negative thoughts captive and make them obey You. And, Lord, help me to stop worrying and to start worshipping You more and more every day.

Do It

Martin Luther once said about worries, "You can't stop the birds from flying, but you can stop them from making a nest in your hair." Take your worries captive!

Day 29

His Word is trustworthy;
it gives us something tangible to hold on to
when we are stepping out in faith.

Today's Verse

Psalm 34:4–5 *"I sought the Lord, and he answered me; he delivered me from all my fears. Those who look to him are radiant; their faces are never covered with shame."*

Read About It

Do you constantly worry about what others think of you? Do you feel inferior and ashamed but don't know what to do about it? I spent the first 26 years of my life like that, searching for ways to feel good about myself. Even with diets, degrees, possessions, jobs, a husband, and children, feelings of inferiority plagued me. After I became a Christian, God started helping me to look to Him for my worth and identity and freeing me from a frantic need to please people. Today's verse tells about this exciting process.

Think About It

David wrote Psalm 34 after he made a bad mistake and was overwhelmed with shame. Let's explore what David says in today's verse to discover how to cooperate with the Lord as he delivers us from feelings of shame.

"I sought the Lord." Whether you are suffering from shame over a mistake you made or you feel like you are a mistake, the answer is still the same: Seek the Lord. Don't just utter a little prayer in passing. Earnestly seek Him daily. When I started writing my prayers and Bible meditations, I began making wonderful progress in overcoming my feelings of inferiority.

But to seek the Lord, we also need to reach out to others for help. In addition to attending church, you will be amazed at the progress you will make if you seek the Lord every week with a prayer partner or Christian mentor. This relationship is even more helpful when you are accountable with this person concerning goals that you have established for yourself. Going to a Christian support group or counselor is also an excellent way to seek the Lord. Many churches have counseling services, some are even free of charge.

"He answered me." When we seek the Lord, God answers us. We can be sure of that, but we must persevere in seeking Him and wait patiently for Him to answer. Before I began having consistent quiet times in writing, my prayers were sporadic and brief. I was easily distracted and couldn't keep my mind on what I was praying. Although God answered some of my prayers, I seldom sensed that He was speaking to me. But now when I pray and study His Word, most of the time I feel God's presence, and I am encouraged by His promises and directed by His commands.

"He delivered me from all my fears." There are two types of fear: The first type is fear of the Lord, which the Bible calls the beginning of wisdom (Proverbs 9:10). This type of fear means to revere God, to be in awe of Him, and to hold Him in the highest regard. The other type of fear causes dread and apprehension. If we truly fear the Lord, our worries will turn to worship.

"Those who look to him are radiant." Have you ever watched two people in love gaze at each other? The love they feel radiates from them. You can see it in their eyes. Neither one of them feels insecure or worried about what others are thinking. Instead, they are rejoicing in the love they feel and the love they see reflected in their loved-one's eyes. The Lord wants us to look to Him like that and see His love for us reflecting from His eyes. He loves us even though we have sinned, we are weak, we make mistakes, we are unworthy of His love. We are His and He wants us to know it.

"Their faces are never covered with shame." It is hard for some people to imagine God's loving gaze directed toward them. When they look to the Lord, they are distracted by someone else's eyes; the parent who rejected them, the husband who betrayed them, or the boss who demeaned them. There is no way to erase, in a day, hurts that have built up over a lifetime, but if you earnestly seek God, He will begin the process of removing your shame. He will comfort you with His Spirit, direct you through His Word, and He will send people into your life to help you to understand how much God really loves you. They will help you to see yourself through God's eyes.

Write About It

Today we are focusing on seeking God. Jeremiah 29:13 tells us: "You will seek me and find me when you seek me with all your heart." Are you seeking God with all your heart? Seeking the Lord doesn't necessarily take a lot of time each day.

During a counseling session, I encouraged Joan to study the Bible every day and she said, "I can't study the Bible 24 hours a day like you do!" I laughed and thanked her for the compliment, though I knew she didn't mean to compliment me.

Then I amazed her by saying that my goal is to study the Bible at least five minutes a day. (I usually study it longer, but five minutes a day is my goal.) Joan made the same mistake that many people make. She didn't realize that to seek God we don't have to pray or study the Bible for a long time every day, but it is important to do both of these things if we are going to seek God daily.

What are you willing to do to seek God more?

1. _____
2. _____
3. _____

What things do you say to excuse yourself from seeking God every day? It is challenging to find time to seek Him, but imagine what you are giving up if you don't! Place a check next to excuses you use. Pray that God will help you to quit making excuses and to start making progress instead.

What Excuses Do You Make?

1. I'm too busy.
2. I have to get to work.
3. I can't find time alone.
4. I forget to pray.
5. I am not disciplined enough.
6. I have too many hurts.
7. It wouldn't help anyway.
8. I'm too overwhelmed.
9. I don't want anyone to know about my problems.
10. Other _____

Pray About It

Reflect on today's verse as you journey from worry to worship. Psalm 34:4–5 *"I sought the Lord, and he answered me; he delivered me from all my fears. Those who look to him are radiant; their faces are never covered with shame."*

Ask God to help you to seek Him more and more every day. Confess excuses you have used for not seeking Him. Pray that He will help you to do the new things you listed.

_____

_____

_____

Lord, thank You that I don't have to do anything to make You love me. You already do. Forgive me for seeking the approval of others. Help me, Lord, to seek You with all my heart and to look to You so my face will never be covered with shame. Help me to feel the love You have for me, so I can base my worth on whose I am not what other people think of me.

Do It

Quit trying to get somewhere in your rocking chair. It's time to get up and seek the Lord!

Day 30

His Word is trustworthy; it gives us something tangible to hold on to when we are stepping out in faith.

Today's Verse

Psalm 32:7 *"You are my hiding place; you will protect me from trouble and surround me with songs of deliverance."*

Read About It

Have you ever had a hiding place—someplace you could go and rest where you wouldn't be bombarded by problems? I did. When I was eight or nine, there was a wooded area in my once-quiet suburban neighborhood outside of Washington, D.C. Every afternoon after school, I would drop off my books at home, give my mom a hug, and then head down to my own private hideaway. In the middle of the woods there was a wonderful tree I loved to climb. Up there, I could see for miles around. It was my hiding place. I felt secure there. No schoolmates to ridicule me. No teachers to harass me. No father to scream at me. I was safe.

Corrie ten Boom had a different kind of hiding place. Her hiding place was the invisible place of safety she found in the midst of a Nazi concentration camp, crammed into an over-crowded, lice-infested dormitory with the murderous ovens nearby. Cruel guards, hungry women, and a dying sister sur-rounded her, yet she felt safe in the Lord's arms.

The Lord was Corrie's hiding place. She knew that if she stayed close to Him through prayer and praise, He would pro-tect her from trouble and surround her with songs of deliver-ance. That didn't mean that the lice would go away, the guards would be kind, or the ovens would close their doors. But the Lord was with her. And she would feel the loving arms of her *Abba* surrounding her.

Think About It

Are you surrounded by trouble? Do you wish you had a hid-ing place to go to—a refuge from the battles you have to fight every day? The psalms are full of word pictures of the Lord—our hiding place, our refuge, and our fortress. Let's look at one of my favorites, Psalm 91:1–4. After each phrase from the Bible, I will share my own paraphrase as if God were speak-ing to us directly.

"He who dwells in the shelter of the Most High will rest in the shadow of the Almighty." Dwell in Me, stay close to Me and I will protect you. I am the Lord Almighty—El-Shaddai, the All-Sufficient One—and I am with you. Praise Me for My presence and My power and you will find the secret of My shelter: I am your hiding place and I go where you go. Praise Me and you will find rest for your soul even during the fiercest combat.

"I will say of the Lord, 'He is my refuge and my fortress, my God, in whom I trust.'" When you praise Me, you will experience a sense of My divine protection. You will feel renewed assurance that I am your God, not some distant deity out there, too busy to concern himself with the things that you are going through. Praising Me builds trust. It allows you to hold fast to My promises and feel secure even in the midst of battle.

"Surely he will save you from the fowler's snare and from the deadly pestilence." I will save you from the devil, who wants to trap you in his lies. And I will save you from death. Because of what Jesus did for you on the cross, you will never die. You will just walk with Me from this life to the next. So rejoice and be glad. Praise Me for My plan, even before you understand it fully.

"He will cover you with his feathers, and under his wings you will find refuge." Praise Me for My purpose for the trials I allow in your life. Praise Me because you know that I allow them only for your good and My glory. Remember the mother eagle that pushes her baby out of the nest to teach him to fly? She hovers over him, just as I hover over you, and she catches him when he falls. I won't let you fall. Trust Me. I will protect you and give you a safe place to go any time you are afraid.

"His faithfulness will be your shield and rampart." I shield you—behind and before—from anything outside of My will. When you praise Me, you will have spiritual eyes to see how faithfully I shield you and bless you. I am blessing you now and I will bless you even more in heaven. I bless you with joy and victory as you go through your battles. And I give you promises to cling to that bring hope. Praise Me and watch your worry transform into worship.

Write About It ✏

On this final day, after we have focused on all six reasons to praise the Lord given in Isaiah 40, I would like to give you a pop quiz. How many of the Six P's do you remember? We praise God for His:

P_____

P_____

P_____

P_____

P_____

P_____

You can find the answers on the next two pages.

Here is an important practical tip: As you race through your days, use the six P's to change your worries into worship. Any time worries attack you, instead of focusing on your worries, try to recall these six P's and start praising the Lord.

Another Way to Wipe Away Worries

During your quiet time, when you have time to deal with your worries in a deeper way, use the Worry to Worship Form. Copy the form in the back of this book to use each time worries strike. Practice using the Worry to Worship Form now by answering each of the questions as you praise the Lord.

Worry to Worship Form

Date_____
What is my worry? _____

God, I praise You for Your presence.
How does God's presence take me from worry to worship?

I praise You for Your power.
How does God's power take me from worry to worship?

I praise You for Your plan.
How does God's plan take me from worry to worship?

I praise You for Your purpose.
How does God's purpose take me from worry to worship?

I praise You for Your prize.
How does God's reward take me from worry to worship?

I praise You for Your promises.
How do God's promises take me from worry to worship?

Pray About It 🙏

Which principles and practical tips in this book have been the most helpful for you? Write a prayer asking God to help you keep using them on your journey from worry to worship.

_____

_____

_____

How have you changed in the past 30 days? Are you worrying less? Are you spending more time in prayer and praise? Are you better able to apply the Word to your worries? Thank God for any progress you have made.

_____

_____

_____

_____

Reflect on today's verse as you journey from worry to worship. Psalm 32:7 *"You are my hiding place; you will protect me from trouble and surround me with songs of deliverance."*
Thank You, Lord, that You are my hiding place. Because I am learning to enter into Your presence with praise, I am no longer at the mercy of my worries. As I praise You, I feel protected and secure, surrounded by Your songs of deliverance instead of my worries and troubles. Help me never to forget the lessons I have learned in the past 30 days about the hiding place I have in You. And help me to continue on my journey from worry to worship as long as I live.

Do It 👣

You know the passwords of praise that open the door to your Hiding Place. Use them!

Leader's Guide for Small Groups

You can start a Worry to Worship group in a Sunday School class, a Bible study, a support group, or with a friend or two in your home. Here are a few guidelines for the leaders:

- This Leader's Guide is designed to provide one weekly session for six weeks. Class meeting times are flexible—anywhere from 30 minutes to two hours.
- A group may consist of 2 to 20 people.
- Emphasize the importance of confidentiality. What is said in the meetings is to stay there.
- Emphasize prayer as an important part of the experience.
- Members are never obligated to share. When asked a question, they may always "pass" if they do not wish to answer.
- In order to encourage openness, ask members to give only positive feedback during the meetings. Honest sharing is encouraged when people are sure that they will not be judged or lectured.
- Every week at the end of the class, encourage members to review the questions that will be asked the next week so that they will be prepared to answer.

Week 1
We praise God for His presence.

1. Ask each person in your class these three questions and share your answer as well:
   - What do you worry about most? (State in one sentence.)
   - When pondering this worry, which verse that we studied this week encourages you most? How?

2. Ask for volunteers to answer one question. After everyone has had the opportunity to answer, if time permits, ask another question.

- Have you ever apologized to someone and felt the walls that had built between you come tumbling down? Explain.
- Do you remember a specific time when you confessed a sin to the Lord and felt the barrier between you begin to crumble? Explain. (Day 4)
- What "Yes, but" have you told God concerning one of His promises? Are you willing to ask God to help you to believe this promise and memorize a corresponding Bible verse to help the truth sink in? (Day 5)
- When have you experienced the Lord leading you through a difficult time in your life? (Day 2)

Week 2

We praise God for His power.

1. Ask each person the following questions:
   - When have you been able to do things or endure things that you never thought possible? (Day 6)
   - How have you been majoring on the minors?
   - What are you going to do to change this and seek God first as Jesus commands in Matthew 6:33? (Day 8)
   - What have you worried about that never happened? (Day 8)
   - How have you been pulling out of your yoke? What are you going to do to yoke yourself back to Jesus? See Matthew 11:28–29. (Day 9)

2. Ask for volunteers to answer these questions:
   - Who made a thanksgiving list? How did it help? (Day 7)
   - Who used another practical tip given this week? How did it help you?

Week 3
We praise God for His plan.

1. Ask each person in your class these questions and answer them yourself:
   - In addition to reading *From Worry to Worship* and attending this class, what new thing are you doing to grow in the Lord? How is this helping you? If you aren't doing anything new, what do you plan to start doing to grow in the Lord? See Colossians 2:7. (Day 11)
   - Which of the word pictures in Day 13 is most helpful to you,? Explain your answer. (Day 13)

2. Ask for volunteers to answer these questions:
   - When have you based your thinking on a misconception about God? What harm did that do? Refer to Susan's Misconceptions in Day 15 to give you some ideas.
   - Have you ever disobeyed God? What happened? (Day 11)

Week 4
We praise God for His purpose.

1. Choose two or three of these questions:
   - What hurt has God used most in your life? How? Refer to the Advantages of Adversity in Day 16 for ideas.
   - What "if only" have you said? How has this "if only" harmed you? Refer to pages Day 17 for ideas.
   - What is Number One on your Miracle List? (Day 18)
   - Which one behavior most encourages you to worry? Refer to Day 19 for ideas.

2. Ask for volunteers to answer one of these questions:
   - Have you made a Victory List? Which goals have you included on it? (Day 20)

- Have you been trying to change something you have no control over? What is happening as a result? (Day 18)

Week 5
We praise God for His prize.

1. Choose two or three of these questions to ask each person and answer yourself:
   - What has God withheld from you that you thought was good, but later realized that it wouldn't have been best? See Psalm 84:11. (Day 22)
   - What lie has the devil been telling you? What is the truth from God's Word that contradicts the lie? Refer to Day 23 for ideas.
   - Which Flesh Builder has given you a sense of false security? What are you going to do to trust in God instead of this? Refer to Day 24 for ideas.
   - How are you running the Rat Race instead of the Right Race? Refer to Day 25 for ideas.

2. Ask for volunteers to answer these questions:
   - How does working as for the Lord help you to do the work that you have to do? See Colossians 3:23–24. (Day 21)
   - Have you ever been persecuted for your faith? Explain. (Day 21)

Week 6
We praise God for His promises.

1. Ask each person two or three of these questions and answer them yourself:

- What situation have you been waiting on the Lord to work out? See Isaiah 40:31 (Day 27)

- What quality do you have in common with a squawking eaglet? What are you willing to do to change? Refer to Day 27 for ideas.

- What are you worrying about today? (Choose a worry from the list in Day 28 or any other worry.) How does the corresponding Bible verse help you to capture that worry? See 2 Corinthians 10:5

- What are you doing to seek God more as a result of this study of *From Worry to Worship*? (Day 29) Are you better able to apply the Word to your worries?

2. Ask for volunteers to answer this question:
   - What comfortable nest have you made for yourself that God may want you to be willing to leave? See Deuteronomy 32:11. (Day 27)

   - When has it felt like God was letting you fall? How did He save you before it was too late? (Day 27)

   - Have you experienced a feeling of insecurity and shame? How is God helping you to overcome that? (Day 29)

3. At the end of the class, encourage class members to share what they have learned and continue their journey from worry to worship by rereading the book, trying different practical tips, and starting their own Worry to Worship group with other friends.